The Black Arc

THE MYTH
MAKERS

By Ian Potter

Published June 2023 by Obverse Books
Cover Design © Cody Schell
Icon © Blair Bidmead
Text © Ian Potter, 2023.

Editors: Paul Driscoll, Stuart Douglas

For Helen, the face that tolerates a thousand quips.

Recently Published

CONTENTS

OVERVIEW

Serial Title: *The Myth Makers*

Writer: Donald Cotton

Director: Michael Leeston-Smith

Original UK Transmission Dates: 16 October 1965 – 6 November 1965

Running Time:	'Temple of Secrets': 24m 45s
	'Small Prophet, Quick Return': 24m 43s
	'Death of a Spy': 25m 38s
	'Horse of Destruction': 24m 25s
UK Viewing Figures:	'Temple of Secrets': 8.3 million
	'Small Prophet, Quick Return': 8.1 million
	'Death of a Spy': 8.7 million
	'Horse of Destruction': 8.3 million

Regular Cast: William Hartnell (the Doctor), Maureen O'Brien (Vicki), Peter Purves (Steven Taylor), Adrianne Hill (Katarina)

Guest Cast: Cavan Kendall (Achilles), Alan Haywood (Hector), Ivor Salter (Odysseus), Francis de Wolff (Agamemnon), Jack Melford (Menelaus), Tutte Lemkow (Cyclops), Max Adrian (King Priam), Barrie Ingham (Paris), Frances White (Cassandra), Jon Luxton (Messenger), James Lynn (Troilus)

Antagonists: Greeks and Trojans.

Novelisation: *Doctor Who: The Myth Makers* by Donald Cotton. **The**

Target Doctor Who Library #97.

Responses:

'Without Homer's strong characters or any spectacular element, the retelling of the tale of Troy was bound to fail unless some other twist could be produced. Unfortunately, neither writer Donald Cotton nor script editor Donald Tosh, nor indeed Producer John Wiles, were able to produce the magic ingredient required.'

[Trevor Wayne, 'Story Review', *Doctor Who: An Adventure in Space and Time* #23]

'We usually have to wait for a lull in the action to discuss anything of importance, but that never happens when the script is this good. We're watching *The Myth Makers* like an episode of modern **Doctor Who** – engaged, enthralled and laughing our asses off.'

[Neil and Sue Perryman, 'The Myth Makers', *Adventures with the Wife in Space*]

SYNOPSIS

Temple of Secrets

The TARDIS has landed outside ancient Troy where the Trojan and Greek heroes **Hector** and **Achilles** are locked in combat. About to win the sword fighting duel, Hector sarcastically invokes Zeus to save Achilles. **The Doctor, Vicki** and **Steven** have been watching inside the TARDIS and when the Doctor approaches to intervene, Hector falls to his knees, mistaking the Doctor for the Greek god. Achilles seizes the opportunity to kill Hector. **Odysseus** arrives with his soldiers and takes the Doctor to the Greek camp in triumph. The Doctor has no choice but to play along as Zeus.

Disguised in Greek costume, Steven leaves Vicki in the TARDIS and heads off to rescue the Doctor, but he is spotted by Odysseus' spy **Cyclops**. Odysseus takes Steven to the camp and brings him before **Agamemnon**, the Greeks' leader. The Doctor suggests Steven be sacrificed at his temple, but Cyclops arrives and through Odysseus passes on the news that the temple has vanished.

Small Prophet, Quick Return

Markings in the ground suggest the TARDIS has been dragged into Troy and Agamemnon now suspects he's been the victim of an elaborate hoax and that the Doctor and Steven are working for the Trojans. The Doctor reveals their true identities as time travellers to Odysseus, who, believing his story, suggests his supernatural knowledge can be used to help the Greeks capture Troy.

The TARDIS has been moved into Troy by **Paris**, the son of the Trojan King **Priam** and brother of Hector. Unable to open the TARDIS, which he assumes is a Greek shrine, Paris wants to put in on public display as a trophy, but his sister, the high priestess **Cassandra,** suggests burning the TARDIS as an offering to the gods. Just as the soldiers are about to set fire to the TARDIS, Vicki comes out and explains she is a time traveller. Priam rejects his daughter's misgivings and offers hospitality to Vicki, renaming her Cressida. These events are witnessed by Odysseus' spy Cyclops.

Steven travels to Troy to rescue Vicki (pretending to be the Greek soldier Diomede) but is confronted by Paris. Despite fighting well, Steven willingly yields and to Paris' surprise asks to be taken prisoner. When he is brought before King Priam, Vicki calls out his name in surprise, which Cassandra says is proof she is a Greek spy.

Death of a Spy

Priam gives Vicki a day to decide if she will provide information and/or use her supernatural powers to help the Trojans defeat the Greeks. If she refuses, she will be sacrificed. She and Steven are locked in the dungeons. Priam's other son, **Troilus**, brings Vicki food and they develop a bond together.

The Doctor, with a day left to come up with a plan to take Troy, suggests a fleet of flying machines could be catapulted into the city. When Odysseus makes clear the Doctor will pilot the first of these machines, the Doctor declares humans weren't made to fly and devises a new plan – the Trojan Horse.

Cyclops visits Steven and Vicki in the dungeons and, having told Vicki they are effectively working against the Doctor now, Steven asks Cyclops to get Odysseus to delay the planned invasion by a day. Cyclops is killed by a Trojan soldier before he can get back to the Greek camp.

The next day, Troilus tells Vicki the Greeks have disappeared and Priam thinks she is responsible. In fact, most of the Greek fleet has sailed away, leaving a handful of men (including Odysseus and the Doctor) behind to hide inside the Trojan Horse. Vicki is taken to see the King, but Paris arrives with the news he has found the Great Horse of Asia and is having it brought into the city.

Horse of Destruction

While Cassandra argues with Paris about his decision to bring the horse into Troy, Vicki sneaks back into the dungeons and releases Steven. Priam and Paris believe she must have summoned the Horse to scare away the Greeks, but Cassandra thinks they have been taken in by Vicki and asks her handmaiden **Katarina** to find 'the sorceress'.

Steven realises he and Vicki can't be seen together. Aware of Vicki's feelings for Troilus, he tells her Troilus must leave the city or die. She returns to the Trojan royal family just after Steven's escape has been discovered by Troilus. The family leave Vicki watched over by Katarina, but later, while Katarina sleeps, Troilus returns to see Vicki. She asks him to go out of the city pretending that he'd find Steven on the plains.

Troilus meets Achilles while searching for Steven and kills him. The Greeks attack and Odysseus and his soldiers enter the palace. Odysseus kills Priam and Paris and takes Cassandra prisoner. Vicki is reunited with the Doctor at the TARDIS, and, after introducing Katarina to the Doctor, she sends her to find Steven. Offscreen, Vicki tells the Doctor she wants to stay in Troy. Steven has been wounded in combat and Katarina and the Doctor are helping him into the TARDIS when Odysseus appears, insisting the Doctor leave his machine with him. When the TARDIS dematerialises with the Doctor,

Steven and Katarina inside, he wonders if the Doctor was Zeus after all.

Out on the plains, a wounded Troilus is watching the city burn when Vicki finds him. She assures him she didn't betray him and says they will build another Troy together.

Inside the TARDIS, the Doctor briefly considers Vicki's fate but his attention quickly turns to finding drugs to heal Steven.

A NOTE ON CHARACTER NAMES

The precise names of several characters featured in *The Myth Makers* (1965) have changed over time, primarily as a result of transliteration from the Greek alphabet of Homer to our Latin alphabet and evolving opinions on how that shift should be handled.

I've chosen to follow the spellings presented in the camera scripts and subsequent novelisation of *The Myth Makers*, which, with one notable exception that we'll return to, tend to favour a Latin C for the Greek letter K.

Diomede's name is actually Diomedes in most texts, but, following the example of Chaucer[1], *The Myth Makers* drops its final S. I'll be doing the same, except when referring to the Diomedes of either Homer or mediaeval writers.

The spelling of other Homeric character names will follow those used in the EV Rieu 20th Century English translations of *The Iliad* and *The Odyssey*.

For convenience I've chosen to call all the different groups allied against the Trojans the 'Greeks'. Strictly speaking this is ahistoric, but

---

[1] In his *Troilus and Cressida* Shakespeare introduces Diomedes with his full name but subsequently refers to him in dialogue only as Diomed. This abbreviated form may indicate Shakespeare's indebtedness to Chaucer or have been adopted as a metrical convenience. Cressida, whose name is a syllable shorter, gets her full name more often. Diomed is also exclusively used for the character listed as Diomedes in the dramatis personae of *Antony and Cleopatra*. The only time Shakespeare uses the form Diomede is in a speech in *Henry VI Part III*. We go to Shakespeare for many things, but not consistent spelling.

the alternative is a preponderance of Myrmidons, Achaeans, Argives, Danaans and Ithacans, which would muddle an already complicated narrative while providing little extra clarity.

The evolution of Cressida's name is sufficiently convoluted to warrant brief discussion within the main text.

THE PROLOGUE

'Like, or find fault: do as your pleasures are: Now good, or bad, 'tis but the chance of war.'

[Shakespeare, *Troilus and Cressida*]

'Please yourselves. '

[Lurcio, **Up Pompeii!**][2]

The Myth Makers is a funny story, literally so for most of its screen time. It's a wittily written and elegantly played comedy that lurches unexpectedly into darkness at its finale, but for all its admirable qualities it also seems to badly fumble the exit of the Doctor's companion Vicki and the introduction of her replacement, Katarina[3].

The Myth Makers is a work that emerges through the collaboration and conflicts of a set of quite disparate characters and, although we can't actually see the finished programme, that conflict shows through.

It's the opening serial of a new production team that hopes to push **Doctor Who** into more adult territory and will find itself facing

---

[2] The 1969 **Up Pompeii!** (1969-75) pilot from which this quote is taken has little in common with *The Myth Makers* beyond being a BBC TV comedy with a period setting, featuring a **Carry On** film lead as its star, Max Adrian in support and a prophetess named Cassandra who says 'woe' a lot.

[3] This judgement is obviously subjective and based on a familiarity with the story through its script and soundtrack alone. Recovery of further moving footage would almost certainly lead to reappraisal.

resistance from those happy with **Doctor Who**'s existing formula[4].

It's also a production which treats its inherited regular cast rather less generously than its guests and seriously unsettles the series' regulars, putting them at odds with the new creative team.

In this **Black Archive**, I'll be examining the source stories that the serial adapted, looking at how they were reworked and how history and legend were engaged with.

I'll be tracing, as far as I can with the available surviving documentation, how *The Myth Makers* developed through production, touching on the innovations it brought to **Doctor Who** and attempting to get a feel of what it was like as a piece of television. I'll also be exploring the primary driving forces behind *The Myth Makers*, most notably two figures then new to **Doctor Who** – Producer John Wiles and writer Donald Cotton. In the absence of extensive fan interviews with either, I'll be looking at their backgrounds and other creative works in an attempt to gain a

---

[4] Examples of resistance to the new regime's ideas within the BBC include, but aren't limited to, opposition to the role of the Doctor being recast and management displeasure at the levels of violence depicted on screen. Smaller scale conflicts which may also suggest a collegiate reluctance to be associated with the programme within the BBC include the blocking of a planned crossover with the popular police drama **Z Cars** (1962-78) in a comic Christmas Day episode and the alleged withdrawal of consent to use characters inspired by the stage play *George and Margaret* written by the BBC's Head of Serials, Gerald Savory. External resistance can be measured by a progressive decline in audience figures and in negative responses to the show in the press and Audience Research Reports (**Doctor Who: The Complete History** (TCH) #6 and #7).

greater understanding of them, and thus their approaches to **Doctor Who**. I'll be using the impressions of them recorded by a third newcomer to the series, story editor Donald Tosh. Tosh, unlike his more elusive colleagues, gifted us with many memories of his involvement with the series over many years of engagement with fandom, though sometimes with less than perfect recall.

Most of the humour in *The Myth Makers* looks after itself, so I'll keep analysis of that to a bare minimum. To paraphrase EB White- 'analysing comedy is like dissecting a frog. Nobody laughs and the frog dies.'

I will occasionally highlight some of the more obscure humour in the text and flag up potential jokes that we might have missed, some of which are sufficiently esoteric they may not actually be there. These will, by definition, not be Donald Cotton's best jokes. If a joke needs either a glossary or careful pointing out it's fallen at the first hurdle of being funny, but if Shakespeare comedies can survive being footnoted to death in critical editions to explain their wordplay, I'm sure it won't hurt *The Myth Makers*.

I'll be offering facts, clearly labelled speculation and a certain amount of myth-busting, while hopefully not seeding too many new myths in the process. I'll try to keep things light where possible but there are portions of this narrative where the story may become a little dense, complicated or obscure, and points where I'm afraid levity won't be appropriate. The past is rarely quite as cosy and straightforward as we'd hope.

CHAPTER 1: FOUNDATIONAL MYTHS

PROFESSOR RUMFORD

It's only a legend.

THE DOCTOR

Yes, I know. And so was Troy until dear old Schliemann dug it up.

[*The Stones of Blood* (1978), episode 2]

There is no history of the Trojan War, only stories[5].

History and story are essentially the same at root, but have rather wandered off from each other, one word retaining the stamp of fact, the other carrying connotations of fantasy[6].

In the case of Troy, what we have in history's place are accreted layers of myth, each retelling built upon earlier versions, often contradicting previously established details or introducing new elements. Any attempt to uncover what lies at the root of the myth has to contend with these archaeological layers of fiction.

Furthermore, while it seems likely the story of the Trojan War has some basis in fact, attempts to identify a 'historical' Troy have been

---

[5] In fact, the Ancient Greek poet Hesiod regarded the fall of Troy and its aftermath as marking the end of the Heroic Age, a mythical era preceding modern history and his present day, the rather less glorious Iron Age – see 'Hesiod's Works and Days'. We are in a period right on the edge of legend.
[6] Both words stem from the Greek 'historia' meaning 'to know' and make their bifurcating ways to us through Latin, Old French and Middle English.

muddied by early archaeological excavations[7].

Hisarlik in Turkey is now widely considered to have been the site of Troy. The site features the remains of impressive walls and is plausibly positioned geographically, situated like the city of Homer's *The Iliad* near the Hellespont[8] and close to a river[9]. Excavation has revealed nine distinct periods of occupation, and there's evidence of the seventh city on the site having been destroyed in fire during the period associated with the fall of Troy. Sadly, the city's first excavator, Heinrich Schliemann, carried out his dig during the 1870s, using a direct and invasive approach now frowned on, and, in his search for artefacts that would help prove the historicity of Homer, dug into soil strata far below the period he had hoped to uncover[10].

Treasures were seized upon that matched Schliemann's expectations, while unregarded evidence was allowed to disperse or build up elsewhere. As a consequence, data from different periods has become jumbled or lost entirely, limiting our ability to build a more complex and reliable picture of the site's overall development.

---

[7] Traditionally, there is more than one Trojan War, with an earlier sacking of the city led by the Greek demigod Heracles occurring during Hesiod's Heroic Age. For this reason, the Trojan War is sometimes referred to as the Trojan Wars, not least in **Doctor Who** – see *The Savages* (1966) and *The Mark of the Rani* (1985). We might, wearing fannish heads, choose to assume the Rani involved herself in Heracles' earlier campaign. There seems to be little evidence of her chemically unbalanced victims on display in *The Myth Makers*.
[8] *The Iliad*, Book XXIII.
[9] The Karamendares in actuality and the Scamander in *The Iliad*.
[10] For a brief summary of Schliemann's approach and how it's now viewed see the Vassar college student blog post, Cistormes, 'A Cautionary Tale'.

Getting a clear picture has been further hindered by Schliemann's own acts of mythogenesis, recounting different stories about the circumstances of his discoveries over time, making him an unreliable source.

Disappointingly, Schliemann, regarded as the father of modern archaeology, has had the fate of many fathers befall him and been found guilty of not doing things the way his children would[11].

Of Mycenaean Men

'Did you ever get to Troy, Drax? Little place in Asia Minor.'

[The Doctor, *The Armageddon Factor* (1979), episode 6]

The siege of Troy is generally believed to have taken place towards the end of the Mycenaean era of Greek prehistory[12], somewhere

---

[11] Schliemann smuggled a collection of copper, gold and silver objects from Hisarlik that he dubbed the Treasures of Priam out of Turkey. These items, not necessarily found together, dated from around a thousand years before the era considered Homeric Troy. (Solly, Meilan, 'The Many Myths of the Man Who "Discovered" – and Nearly Destroyed – Troy'.)

[12] The dominant, expansionist Mycenaean civilisation has been named after the city of Mycenae, which, according to *The Iliad*, was ruled by Agamemnon. Mycenae was also the site Schliemann shifted his attention to after being barred from returning to Hisarlik. Schliemann dubbed the impressive golden death mask he found at Mycenae the Mask of Agamemnon in honour of the hero. Once again modern archaeologists have dated the artefact to a somewhat earlier period (circa 1550-00 BCE).

around 1200 BCE[13]. Excavations at Mycenaean sites have revealed cities surrounded by Cyclopean walls[14], intricate work in gold and bronze and detailed accounting in a script dubbed Linear B which confirms an extensive trading network. Mycenaean culture clearly spread across the Greek mainland and shipwreck evidence confirms trade with both Egypt and modern-day Iraq. The assumption of archaeologists is that Troy, situated at the edge of the Hittite empire, would have been an attractive and presumably wealthy site to conquer[15].

One mooted theory is that Troy's location allowed control of the Dardanelles strait (the modern name of the Hellespont) linking the Mediterranean to the Black Sea, which would have been useful for trade[16].

---

[13] *A History of Greece to 322 BC* by NGL Hammond, one of a number of books referred to by Donald Cotton in his research for *The Myth Makers*, goes into some detail about the traditionally assigned dates of the Trojan War in Appendix 2. A full list of Cotton's cited research materials can be found in the Appendix.

[14] Cyclopean walls are ones made from large roughly hewn limestone blocks, usually uncemented, with any gaps in the stonework filled by smaller limestone pieces. The name derives from a tradition of such walls having been built by the Cyclopes, a race of one-eyed giants we first learn of in Hesiod. Mythologically, the Cyclopes are generally associated with manufacture, with the lone shepherd Cyclops of Homer's *The Odyssey* being something of an outlier.

[15] Heneage, James, *The Shortest History of Greece*, pp9-10.

[16] This possibility is raised by Starr, Chester G, *The Origins of Greek Civilisation 1100-650 BC*, p51, another of the texts used by Cotton when researching *The Myth Makers*.

This is the rationale for the siege of Troy that *The Myth Makers* puts in the mouth of Menelaus.

AGAMEMNON

Now, you knew perfectly well what she was like before you married her... It becomes a question of honour to get her back. Of family honour, you understand?

MENELAUS

Not to mention the trade routes through the Bosphorous, of course!

AGAMEMNON

What have they got to do with it?

MENELAUS

It isn't enough for you that you control the Achaean League, is it? Now you want to take over Asia Minor as well: and King Priam of Troy stands in your way.[17]

---

[17] 'Temple of Secrets'. The use of the phrase 'Achaean League' here is strictly speaking anachronistic, although Homer does often refers to the Greek forces collectively as Achaeans in *The Iliad*. The historical Achaean League was a loose confederacy of Greek city states first formed in the fifth century BCE.

CHAPTER 2: SOURCE TEXTS

VICKI

But Mike, that's all mythology. The Trojan war didn't really happen, did it?

MIKE

Oh, it happened alright, excavations have proved that. Only, of course, it didn't happen quite as Homer said it did. That was mostly myth as you say. But there must have been a basis for the myths, don't you see? They don't grow out of nothing. I think the men who carried off the DR. were the original mythmakers: the men whose exploits were magnified by later generations until they seemed heroic and superhuman.[18]

Two of the most oft repeated claims made about *The Myth Makers* are that it's based on the plot of *The Iliad*[19] by Homer and that it uses the story of Troilus and Cressida to write Vicki out of the series.

Both these claims are wrong.

---

[18] Extract from Donald Cotton's 1965 handwritten draft for *The Myth Makers* episode 1, under the title 'Deus Ex Machina'. The character of Steven was still being developed at this point and Mike was one of his earlier potential names.
[19] The title indicates it's a work relating to Ilion, an alternative name for Troy.

The Iliad

The Iliad is a work in verse[20], an epic poem originally either sung or recited. It's believed to have been composed around the eighth century BCE and actually only covers only a short period towards the end of 10-year siege of Troy.

To offer a very brief synopsis, it begins with Troy already besieged and King Agamemnon of Mycenae being persuaded to return a local woman called Chryseis to her father Chryses, a priest of Apollo. Chryseis had been taken by force as a prize of war to be Agamemnon's concubine, and her return is only agreed after the god Apollo visits plague on the Greek camp. Piqued by the loss of his sexual property, Agamemnon takes Briseis in her place, a woman similarly given to Achilles, the greatest of the Greeks' warriors. In protest, an angry Achilles refuses to continue fighting the Trojans and entreats the god Zeus to ensure Agamemnon and his forces are humbled in battle.

Despite heroic fighting by Diomedes, who appears to be the greatest Greek warrior after Achilles, the Greeks begin to suffer defeats and the besieged Trojans start pressing their advantage and attack the Greek camp.

Patroclus, a close friend of Achilles, dresses in Achilles' armour to go into battle, hoping the sight of the great warrior apparently returned

---

[20] Composed in dactylic hexameter, though that need not detain us here. The use of verse leads to a preponderance of stock phrases that fit the meter that are often repeated, often in the form of epithets given the various heroes. This verbal tic, preserved in most modern translations, is parodied several times in *The Myth Makers*.

will unsettle the Trojans. Unfortunately, Patroclus is slain by Hector, the son of King Priam of Troy, leading Achilles to re-enter the fray to avenge him. Achilles kills Hector after chasing him three times around the walls of Troy on foot. In an act showing extreme disrespect for his vanquished foe, Achilles then proceeds to drag Hector's body behind his chariot for several days. King Priam pleads for the return of his son's body and, moved by his grief, Achilles relinquishes Hector's remains[21].

There's very little here that finds it way directly into the plot of *The Myth Makers*, though there's much that will inform it. *The Iliad* finishes some time before Troy falls and, although my brief summary glosses over it, the story involves a fair deal of intercession from the gods of Olympus.

Homer is not, in fact, the sole author of the tale of Troy, and this is why he is only telling a portion of it. The larger story is related in his era through a series of poetic works referred to as the Epic Cycle, now almost wholly lost. Luckily, although only tiny quoted fragments of them remain in other works, we know the broad content of these poems through later commentary.

One of these lost works, *The Cypria*, relates events in the war preceding *The Iliad*, and two others, known as *The Little Iliad* and *Iliupersis*, deal with the construction of the Trojan Horse and its use

---

[21] Homer, *The Iliad*, EV Rieu, trans, pp23-459.

in the sack of Troy[22].

The earliest version of the Trojan Horse story that's survived to reach us is a brief account in Homer's *The Odyssey*[23], the story of Odysseus' long journey home after the war. The Horse is later alluded to in Euripides' tragedy *The Trojan Women* (first performed in 415 BCE), a play which also introduces us to the idea that Cassandra, the daughter of Priam (mentioned only in passing in *The Iliad*) is a seer cursed to never be believed. The first detailed account we have comes centuries later in the *Posthomerica* of Quintus of Smyrna, a retelling of much of the Trojan Epic Cycle dated to the late second or third century CE which also features Cassandra's cursed gift.

Other Truths

'The algorithm generates probabilities, based on crisis points, anomalies, anachronisms, keywords – blue box, Doctor...

[...] San Martino, Troy, multiples for New York, three possible

---

[22] It's not entirely clear whether the other poems of the Epic Cycle precede and influence Homer's work or follow and are informed by it, though most scholars presume the latter. In correspondence with the production team, Cotton refers to these works as 'the Cyprian Epics', an overarching description now rarely used.

[23] Although *The Iliad* and *The Odyssey* are attributed to Homer and utilise some of the same stock phrases, the styles of the two works are markedly different and they are usually believed to have been developed orally over a long period by multiple writer-performers, before being set down in writing. The Wooden Horse story is told by the bard Demodocus in Book VIII of *The Odyssey* (Homer, *The Odyssey*, EV Rieu, trans, pp135-36) though Homer gives us only a short summary of his performance.

versions of Atlantis...'

[Jac, *The Magician's Apprentice* (2015)]

The Greek myths, much like **Doctor Who**'s explanations of them[24], do not exist in just one form, and ancient writers (and presumably audiences) seem to have been happy to accept varying contradictory treatments of the same tales. There are, for example, celebrated works based on the Trojan War in which Helen, whose abduction is usually held to have begun the war, never even went there[25]. Myth was a foundation to build on, and Homer's work in turn served as a foundation for other writers.

The most influential of Homer's reinterpretations comes centuries later (circa 30-19 BCE) in *The Aeneid* of the Roman author Virgil. It's a story linking itself to events of *The Odyssey* that popularises the use of Ulysses, the Roman name for Odysseus, which incorporates and expands on the stories of the Trojan Horse and Cassandra's curse[26]. It's *The Aeneid* which, crucially for the plot of *The Myth Makers*, takes the minor character Aeneas from *The Iliad* and makes him the mythical founder of a new Trojan homeland. Aeneas ultimately sets up a Trojan colony at Alba Longa in Italy, the reputed birthplace of Romulus and Remus, ensuring the foundation of Rome and allowing Romans to consider themselves descended from heroic

---

[24] **Doctor Who** has generously offered viewers a choice of rationalisations for both the Minotaur and Atlantis.
[25] *The Oxford History of the Classical World* cites a sixth century BCE poem by Stesichorus, Euripides' play *Helen* and Herodotus, finding it a more plausible version of the myth Homer chose to ignore (p80). The Helen fought over at Troy in these treatments is a phantom.
[26] Virgil, *The Aeneid*, WF Jackson Knight, trans, pp51-74.

stock[27]. It is this that Vicki glancingly refers to in episode 4:

TROILUS

It's my cousin!

VICKI

Your cousin?

TROILUS

Aeneas. Oh, if only he'd come sooner.

VICKI

That's it!

TROILUS

What?

VICKI

He'll help us.

TROILUS

But, there's nothing left.

VICKI

There is. There's us. We can start again. With your cousin's help, we can build another Troy.[28]

---

[27] The story of the Trojan Horse is told here by Aeneas to Dido, Queen of Carthage, but at far greater length and incorporating many details that become part of later tradition.
[28] 'Horse of Destruction'.

Some fan commentators have assumed Troilus and Vicki will be attempting to rebuild Troy where it once stood, but the introduction of Aeneas makes it fairly clear this isn't the script's intention[29]. Going away with Aeneas is certainly more attractive than lingering in the rubble and being taken off by the Greeks, the fate that awaits the characters of Euripides' *The Trojan Women*. Vicki's decision here might suggest she has some familiarity with Aeneas' story, but, if so, her knowledge is slightly patchy[30]. In both *The Iliad* and *The Aeneid*, Troilus is already long dead and Cressida is nowhere to be found.

Troilus is mentioned only once in the entire *The Iliad*, when Priam laments in Book XXIV that he 'had the best sons in the broad realm of Troy. Now all of them are gone, the godlike Mestor, Troilus, that happy charioteer, and Hector, who walked among us like a god...'[31] No cause of death is established, but beyond Homer, Troilus is traditionally depicted as a beautiful Trojan youth ambushed and slain by Achilles during an earlier period of the war. There's only a

---

[29] The Time Space Visualiser blog presumes Vicki is staying in 'Greece' and speculates on possible futures for Vicki based on other literary works (suggesting she's likely to die of leprosy or be enslaved by the Greeks) without considering the significance of Aeneas. Both Trevor Wayne and J Jeremy Bentham assume Vicki faces almost certain death as a result of staying behind at the ruins of Troy, with Wayne dismissing the talk of founding a new Troy as 'very optimistic indeed' in *An Adventure in Space and Time* #20, (pp5 and 7). Troilus and Cressida explicitly leave with Aeneas to found Rome in Donald Cotton's 1985 novelisation, but we can't be 100% confident this was the intention in the 1960s.

[30] Quite plausible given the knowledge of history Vicki displays in *The Chase* (1965).

[31] *The Iliad*, p444. The translator EV Rieu has chosen 'charioteer' to cover an unspecified association with horses in the original.

passing mention of this in a summary of the Epic Cycle's *Cypria*[32] but in later representations and interpretations of the story, Achilles overwhelms and beheads him, with a sexual element read into the hero's pursuit of the boy[33].

This may surprise contemporary audiences, but it has to be remembered the Greek heroes are not 'heroic' figures in the modern sense. They are driven, flawed figures with huge passions that separate them from ordinary men.

Furthermore, while it's hard to detect in *The Iliad*, where the trading of women seems to be at the root of much of the conflict, pederastic love was openly celebrated in Archaic and Classical Greek culture, and many later Greek and Roman authors matter-of-factly depict Achilles' friend Patroclus as his sexual partner[34]. Achilles and Patroclus are certainly considered lovers by Thersites in

---

[32] Proclus, *Chrestomathia*. Later Classical texts, also wholly or partly lost, expand on the death of Troilus, relating his youth and beauty. *The Aeneid* provides us with a fuller account, though obviously at some remove from the earliest versions.

[33] The clearest textual example of this appears in Servius' commentary on *The Aeneid* in the fifth century CE, but the death of Troilus was a popular motif in Classical art and many depictions, in which a boyish Troilus is overwhelmed by an adult Achilles, are interpreted as having erotic intent. For further reading, see Lambrou, Ioannis L, 'Homer and Achilles' Ambush of Troilus: Confronting the Elephant in the Room', *Greece & Rome*, #65.1, pp7-85, Brouwers, Josho, 'Achilles' Slaying of Troilus', and Parada, Carlos, 'Troilus'.

[34] Plato's *Symposium* involves some discussion of the precise nature of their sexual love. Contrarily, Xenophon's *Symposium* puts forward an argument they were simply good friends. This appears to have been what fourth century BCE Athenian drinking parties were like.

Shakespeare's *Troilus and Cressida*[35], and it is probably this tradition Donald Cotton alludes to when discussing Achilles in his 1984 novelisation of *The Myth Makers*:

> 'He was more lightly armoured than Hector: but I couldn't help feeling that this was not so much a matter of military requirement, as of pride in the displaying of his perfectly proportioned body. He had that look of Narcissistic petulance one so often sees on the faces of health fanatics, or on male models who pose for morally suspect sculptors. I believe the Greeks have a word for it nowadays.'[36]

Luckily for Vicki, Troilus doesn't stay dead in later iterations of the tale of Troy, and one might perhaps assume Vicki is working from a knowledge of Shakespeare's play *Troilus and Cressida* for a sense of what a future with Troilus and Aeneas might hold. There are only two problems to contend with here. Firstly, Aeneas barely features in the play at all, which, takes his fate no further forward than the action of *The Iliad*. Secondly, Shakespeare's story has Cressida leaving Troilus for the Greek Diomedes, the role the recently departed Steven takes on in *The Myth Makers*.

Vicki's fate in the TV show is a complete subversion of the established Troilus and Cressida narrative.

A Short History of Troilus and Cressida

Cressida is a mediaeval invention whose seed appears to be a character from *The Iliad* we came across in our earlier summary,

---

[35] Act V, scene I, p263 in the Arden edition. Thersites has, however, been declared a slanderer earlier in the play.
[36] Cotton, Donald, *The Myth Makers*, p15.

Briseis, the woman given to Achilles as a war prize who is then taken by Agamemnon to compensate for his loss of Chryseis.

In the 12th century CE, the French author Benoît de Sainte-Maure, created his own reinterpretation of the Trojan War story in the *Roman de Troie*, a work building on Latin versions of now lost Greek retellings[37].

In Benoît de Sainte-Maure's version, Briseis is renamed Briseida[38], a young Trojan woman in a loving relationship with Troilus (here both fully adult and alive). Briseida is now given to the Greeks by her father to ensure her future safety rather than forcibly taken as in *The Iliad*. While in the Greek camp, Briseida falls in love with the Greek hero Diomedes. This angers Troilus who seeks revenge. Diomedes and Troilus engage in combat and Diomedes is seriously injured. It is the sight of Diomedes' wounds that moves Briseida to choose life with him over Troilus[39]. Briseida's story ends here with her lamenting her fickle nature, though the men's narratives continue. Diomedes

---

[37] These are the alleged eyewitness accounts of the Trojan War by Dares of Phrygia and Dictys of Crete. Dictys prolongs the life of Troilus, making him an adult warrior active in the war after the death of Hector (Book 4 – *Posthomerica*). He now has his throat cut on Achilles' orders as a prisoner defeated in combat. Further background detail can be found in *The Roman de Troie by Benoît de Saint-Maure*, pp5-8.

[38] Briseida derives from the accusative rather than nominative form of Briseis, meaning daughter of Brises (see page xi of Stephen A Barney's introduction to the Norton Critical edition of Chaucer's *Troilus and Criseyde*), though in this telling she becomes the daughter of the Trojan priest Calcas.

[39] The Troilus-Briseida-Diomedes triangle is covered between p202 and p294 of *The Roman de Troie*.

will go on to be reconciled with his wife after returning from the war[40] and Troilus to be slain, as usual, by Achilles[41].

This new story is reworked by de Sainte-Maure's contemporary Guido delle Colonne, in the *Historia Destructionis Troiae*, but it's not until the early 14th century CE that Briseida becomes Criseida[42] in *Il Filistrato*, Giovanni Boccaccio's treatment of the tale.

Boccaccio's *Il Filistrato* then informs Chaucer's *Troilus and Criseyde* (c1350 BCE), which in turn influences *The Recueil of the Histories of Troy* by Raoul Lefèvre, a French version of the Troy story that, in a translation by William Caxton, became the first work printed in the English language in 1474[43]. Homer, Chaucer and Lefèvre are all believed to have been used by Shakespeare in the writing of his *Troilus and Cressida*, circa 1602 BCE[44].

We've come quite a long way from Homer's 800-700BCE, and further again from the traditionally assigned date of the fall of Troy, 1184

---

[40] *The Roman de Troie*, p390.

[41] Troilus' now heroic death occurs on p304, as he faces multiple Greek warriors in combat. Despite this, his throat is still ignominiously cut by Achilles.

[42] EV Rieu's footnotes to *The Iliad* tentatively suggest a link between Cressida and Chryseis (pp464-65). Boccaccio may have introduced the C to Briseida to rationalise and conflate Briseis and Chryseis.

[43] Lefèvre and Caxton's treatment of Troilus and Cressida (though it preserves the name Briseida while acknowledging Chaucer) occupies pp402-24 of DM Smith's modern English version of the *Recueil*.

[44] Further likely Shakespearean sources, including Lydgate's *Troy Book*, are discussed in the Arden edition of *Troilus and Cressida* (pp22-38) which also supplies this approximate dating (p17).

BCE[45], to arrive at Troilus and Cressida.

Boccaccio, Chaucer and Shakespeare's retellings emphasise the procuring of Cressida for the Greeks by the character Pandarus[46] (who shares the name with a minor Trojan archer in *The Iliad*) from whose name we derive the word 'pander'[47]. In Shakespeare's play, despite Cressida being a title character, she's almost entirely absent from the last act where the broader story derived from *The Iliad* takes centre stage.

Though it may have passed most of its audience by, when **Doctor Who** pairs Vicki and Troilus it is creating an entirely new myth.

That this has gone largely unnoticed is perhaps unsurprising[48], as most of the programme's 1960s child audience was probably familiar only with the broadest strokes of the stories of Troy, and likely knew of *Troilus and Cressida* solely by title, mentally filing it alongside *Romeo and Juliet* and *Antony and Cleopatra* as a Shakespeare play about love.

---

[45] The date for the fall of Troy first proposed by the third century BCE scholar Eratosthenes.

[46] Pandaro in Boccaccio and variously Pandar, Pandare, Pandares and Pandarus in Chaucer.

[47] *The Shorter Oxford English Dictionary* defines a pander as both 'a go between in clandestine amours; a male bawd or procurer' and more generally as 'one who ministers the baser passions or evil designs of others' (p151). The unfortunate Troilus also has a word coined in his honour – 'troilism'.

[48] Cotton's novelisation of *The Myth Makers* does little to disabuse us of the notion Troilus and Cressida are preordained to stay together:

"'It's a very pretty name," said Vicki.

Despite a handful of acclaimed productions, notably that of John Barton at the Royal Shakespeare Company, the play was (and is) little staged. It has a large cast and a sour tone and has long been regarded as one of Shakespeare's 'problem plays', mixing tragedy and comedy, rather like *The Myth Makers*, in a way some critics and audiences find unsatisfactory. [49]

It is, however, a shame to see *The Myth Makers* disparaged by early 1980s fandom for lacking the 'magic ingredient' of a 'twist' when, by reversing the expected resolution of the love of Troilus and Cressida in its final episode, it takes a huge liberty with its source stories.

The Problem of Vicki

So why does *The Myth Makers* subvert the Troilus and Cressida narrative?

The short answer is – we'll never know, but probably by accident.

The earliest full synopsis from writer Donald Cotton features no

---

"Very well, then – Cressida it shall be."
"Thank you," said Vicki, "that's who I am, then." And from that instant she was lost forever, and at last found her proper place in Time and History! For we are the prisoners of our names, more than ever we are of what we imagine to be our destinies. They shape our lives, and mould our personalities, until we fit them.'
(Cotton, *The Myth Makers*, pp64-65.)

[49] 'Problem plays' is a critical label that's been attached to works of Shakespeare adjudged by critics to have an inconsistency of tone, defying clear categorisation as either comedy or tragedy. *Troilus and Cressida* offers the additional issue of classification by also looking a bit like one of Shakespeare's history plays. See Brooke, Michael, 'Shakespeare's Problem Plays'.

reference to Troilus or Cressida and ends with Vicki leaving in the TARDIS alongside the Doctor and Mike.

It's generally been presumed that the Troilus subplot developed after producer John Wiles chose not to renew Maureen O'Brien's contract. As an orphan from the future who'd lost her father en route to a new life on a colony world, Vicki had no clearly delineated home to return to so a rationale had to be devised for her remaining in ancient Troy. Following the template set by Susan, the first companion to depart the series, it was decided she was to fall in love and choose to settle in a time that was not her own[50].

However, given Cressida's literary reputation as an unfaithful lover it feels odd to identify Vicki with her and romantically pair her with Troilus. It becomes decidedly odder when we consider Diomede, Cressida's other literary lover, is the name adopted by the Doctor's male travelling companion. It's a curious choice for a happy ending.

The ruins of ancient Troy seem a far less hospitable environment in which to leave a young companion than Susan's ruined future London. In the future, the invaders had been defeated and the world was about to be rebuilt. In the Mycenaean past, Troy has been destroyed and its people defeated. Not even the arrival of Aeneas to

---

[50] Vicki was only the fourth regular character to leave the series. Where Ian and Barbara were adults with agency and an obvious home to return to, both Vicki and Susan were written as vulnerable teenagers without clear homes. Their falling in love and choosing to stay with a romantic protector essentially ends both their adventures and their childhoods. It's **Doctor Who**'s own peculiar, practical variation on 'the problem of Susan', identified by critics of CS Lewis' **Narnia** books – working out **how** to write out your young adventurer, rather than wrestling with the **why** of its doing.

conveniently whip Troilus and Cressida away into another epic poem (and drama of doomed love) can lift the mood much[51].

I think the apparent oddity of this decision arises because the established consensus on how it came about is slightly out. *The Myth Makers'* scripts were commissioned in two batches, the second set not being approved until after the delivery of the first pair on 4 June 1965.

From evidence we'll explore later, we now know that Vicki being renamed as Cressida and being quite taken with Troilus was already part of these first two scripts. The second set followed on 25 June and 28 July, and while no early drafts survive, it seems safe to assume they built on the setup established and the Troilus and Cressida subplot existed in advance of the decision to write out Vicki.

In a 2011 interview, Donald Tosh remembered:

> 'If we had known, when we'd first commissioned Donald to write *The Myth Makers*, that Maureen was leaving, then that would have been integrated into the script more smoothly, but that didn't happen. Instead, I was just suddenly informed that Maureen was going, and she had to be written out. Well, when I told Donald, almost straight off, he pointed out we had a way we could do it, as we'd already written this Troilus and Cressida thing into the story; we'd just have Cressida

---

[51] Troilus and Vicki are presumably fated to lurk in the periphery of Virgil's *The Aeneid* and end up witnessing the story most famously told in English by Christopher Marlowe in *Dido, Queen of Carthage*. Given the complete lack of a planned story arc for Vicki, it's an amusing coincidence (to me at least), that we first meet her on the planet Dido and she ends up travelling with Aeneas.

leave with Troilus instead of leaving with Diomede, the name Steven was using in the story, as originally planned.'[52]

We have to be careful about taking Tosh's word as gospel here – these are events recalled at some distance and some of Tosh's recollections of his **Doctor Who** work are demonstrably faulty[53] – but this seems to confirm the Troilus and Cressida storyline was conceived before Vicki's departure was decided on.

This decision seems to have come very late in the day, with the choice to not extend Maureen O'Brien's contract appearing to have been taken in early September, some months after Cotton delivered his scripts[54].

Further evidence that O'Brien's departure was not planned far in advance can be found in Terry Nation's draft scripts for the serial that followed *The Myth Makers*, delivered at some point between

---

[52] Stevens, Alan, 'Donald Tosh Interview'.

[53] Tosh, for instance, remembered Nation's scripts for *The Daleks' Master Plan* being severely under length and in need of extensive input from him – something proven incorrect when Nation's first drafts came to light. (Cooray Smith, James, *The Black Archive #2:The Massacre*, p21). No dishonesty will have been intended; such inconsistencies naturally arise from the combination of human memory and a storyteller's instincts.

[54] Maureen O'Brien and Peter Purves had both been contracted for a run of episodes that would have taken them to the end of *The Myth Makers* on 24 May 1965. On 3 September the option of extending Peter Purves' contract was taken up while the option on Maureen O'Brien's was not. By this point *The Myth Makers* was well into production, with location filming having already taken place.

mid-July and early September 1965[55].

Nation's scripts refer to the new companion, Katarina, as Vicki right up to the moment of her death four episodes in. Nation is clearly aware there is to be a new companion by the time he writes his third episode, indicating he's expecting rewrites to be needed to make it appropriate for Vicki's replacement. In episode 4, 'The Traitors', Nation's script for the death of 'Vicki' requests the insertion a eulogy touching on what has been established about the new character.

Questioned in 1984 over why Katarina hadn't been integrated into *The Myth Makers'* scripts earlier, Donald Cotton recalled only being asked to make changes to his final episode:

> 'I was told to write out Vicki and bring in Katarina. In fact, half of the last episode, the fourth episode of *The Myth Makers*, was devoted to establishing Katarina for the next adventure. It wasn't my idea. I was just told that Vicki was leaving and I must write in someone else.'[56]

There's textual evidence in the camera script, which we'll return to, that supports Cotton having written Katarina's introduction and Vicki's departure after delivering his initial draft of 'Horse of Destruction', though it's now unclear how much of that work remains in the final version.

The question of how Cotton's scripts originally intended to resolve

---

[55] This approximate dating is extrapolated from the serial's 16 July commissioning date and Wiles' script notes to Nation dated 7 September (Howe, David H, Mark Stammers and Stephen James Walker, *Doctor Who: The Handbook – The First Doctor*, p80).
[56] Transcribed from *Myth Makers #79 Bonus Feature*.

Vicki's burgeoning attraction to Troilus still remains. One imagines Troilus would have interpreted her leaving with Steven as romantic inconstancy and that this would have been the birth of another myth – the mediaeval tale of Cressida – but there's an additional possibility worth considering.

As transmitted, *The Myth Makers* ends on a cliffhanger with Steven wounded in combat and being tended to by Katarina, and it's generally taken that this is a consequence of Terry Nation's first draft of the next episode requesting Steven being seriously in need of medical attention at its opening[57]. It's most likely that Steven's injury was written into 'Horse of Destruction' at Nation's request, but it's also just possible this was a dramatic situation already devised for *The Myth Makers* that happily aligned with Nation's plans. Could Cotton have been planning to play on the pre-Chaucerian versions of the Troilus story in which, after seeing Diomede wounded in combat, Cressida attends to his injuries and chooses him over Troilus? If so, the original scheme for *The Myth Makers* would have seen Vicki becoming attached to Troilus just as she is onscreen, only to feel compelled to leave him and tend to the injured Steven at the climax of episode 4. This would then mirror *The Myth Makers'* primary narrative, presenting a plot that seems to offer up the foundation of a traditional story rather than one that chooses to flip it on its head.

Referencing mediaeval texts in a family tea-time adventure may seem an esoteric choice at this remove, but there is much that might

---

[57] 'The Nightmare Begins', episode 1 of *The Daleks' Master Plan* (at this point simply listed as 'Twelve Part Dalek Segment' on the script front). Steven is 'Stephen' in Nation's scripts.

now seem obscure in *The Myth Makers*, and both Donald Cotton and John Wiles appear to have taken an interest in the mediaeval period. This wasn't, after all, the first time Donald Cotton had written about Cressida.

CHAPTER 3: THE ENGAGING MR COTTON

'I was engaged to the script editor's sister.'

[Donald Cotton.][58]

'He was known as the most engaging man around town, because every time he wanted to go to bed with someone he'd ask them to marry him.'

[Hilary Wright.][59]

Before exploring the texts of *The Myth Makers* in detail it's worth taking a little time to examine its principal author.

Donald Henry Cotton was born near[60] Nottingham on 26 April 1928, the son of Professor Harry Cotton, the distinguished and respected head of Electrical Engineering at Nottingham University and a mother described by Cotton's wife Hilary Wright as 'neurotic and over possessive'[61]. According to Wright, Cotton's father, while a

---

[58] This is Cotton's answer to the question of how he came to write for **Doctor Who** when interviewed at the DWASocial 5 convention held in 1984. The interview is available as a bonus feature on *Myth Makers #79*.

[59] Transcribed from Testro, Lucas, *Myth Maker: The Lost Legacy of Donald Cotton*, episode 2.

[60] According to Cotton's 1969 biography in the programme of *My Dear Gilbert* at the Worthing Connaught Theatre. His father's address is given as Mapperley Street in Nottingham in the mid-1930s, but local press places him in Gunthorpe, a small village near Nottingham, in 1952, so this may well be where Cotton grew up.

[61] Testro, Lucas, 'Man Out of Time', DWM #581, p25. More detail on Professor Cotton's career can be found in Crewe, ME, 'The Met Office Grows Up: In War and Peace'.

popular and gregarious figure, was stand-offish with his son, and the boy seems to have grown up a solitary, guarded child. Cotton went to the local Southwell Minster Grammar School, a school which, having historically trained boy choristers, retained a strong music tradition. Reading his school's annual magazine, Cotton seems to have made no special impact during his time there, unlike his father, who as the school's governor regularly appears in its pages.

After school, Cotton attended Nottingham University, initially choosing to read zoology[62] before transferring to studying English and psychology. During his student years Cotton wrote for university 'Rag' shows and became increasingly involved with drama groups, and there are references to what appears to be him acting in university productions in 1944[63] and 1946[64].

1946 also finds Cotton winning the university's Kirke White poetry prize with a piece entitled 'The Cornfield'[65].

---

[62] Preddle, Jon, 'Myth Maker: Donald Cotton Obituary'.

[63] 'Two Student Plays. Presented at Nottm. University College', *Nottingham Journal*, 18 November 1944. The report remarks that Donald Cotton is 'particularly well cast' in John Drinkwater's short play *X=0*. *X=0* was an anti-war play from 1917 that had escaped censure by dealing with the Siege of Troy rather than directly addressing the Great War. Cotton performing with the 'Nottingham University College Drama Society' at just 16 is striking. However, it appears he may have had an extended period of involvement with the university, possibly due to his father's position there.

[64] A Production of JB Priestley's *When We Are Married*. 'Marital Comedy: UCDS Present Priestley Play', *Nottingham Journal*, 1 March 1946.

[65] See the Worldcat library entry for 'The Cornfield'.

Early Stages

The 1947-48 edition of the Southwell Minster school magazine gives an extended writeup of Cotton's many extracurricular activities as he enters what the magazine states will be his eighth year at the university [66]. By now, he's on the Social and Common Rooms committees, is president of the social society 'Kaleidosoc' for which he writes and produces plays, is secretary of the Entertainments Society and on the committee of the Dramatic Society[67].

In 1949 Cotton was one of four university players to join the company of the Nottingham Playhouse, appearing in *The Merchant of Venice, By Candle Light*[68] and a production of *Othello* staged at the Embassy Theatre in London as part of a season celebrating regional rep theatre[69]. It's not long after this that Cotton gives up his university studies to train as an actor, securing a place at the Guildhall School of Music and Drama. While at the Guildhall, he mounts *On the Level,* a revue in which it's clear the comic voice we're familiar with from his **Doctor Who** work is already emerging:

> 'On the whole, the sketches and lyrics by Donald Cotton, with their sharp satire and ingenious puns, were good, if one takes

---

[66] While this is definitely our Donald Cotton, the numbers here can't be quite right, as they'd have Cotton heading to university at about 12 or 13. I suspect this is a typo and 'year' should read 'term'.
[67] 'The Southwellian', vol 6.2, p20.
[68] 'The Playhouse', *Nottingham Journal*, 26 July 1949.
[69] 'Playhouse Farewells', *Nottingham Journal*, 15 June 1949. Cotton played the small role of Sailor in *Othello*, a character given two lines in Act I, scene 3.

no offence at long words.'[70]

About a year later, with school friend Raymond Long, who had played organ at the Minster as his musical collaborator, Cotton devised his first treatment of the Troy story, entitled *Pandarus, or the Ilium Smile*. The play was a light opera, staged by Guildhall students in 1951[71]. The Nottinghamshire newspaper *The Newark Advertiser* detected 'something of Gilbert and Sullivan about it'[72] though one of its later actors, the acerbic diarist Angus Mackay, felt too little of their influence was apparent:

> 'The people are all no doubt honest, respectable and hard-working, but cannot work at rehearsing and seem to have no sense of theatre at all. This is going to be a Large Disaster. How have they got a run-thro? Ran through my songs, absurdly old-fashioned inferior Gilbert and Sullivan with a dash of Roger Quilter. Absurd.'[73]

Mackay also appears to have been less than impressed by Donald Cotton in particular a couple of days later:

> 'Was asked to luncheon at St. Anne's, but had to rush away though the company was fascinating, in pursuit of a Pandarus rehearsal in the wilds of Highgate. It was a very hot close day, and I was not dressed for what was practically mountaineering. I wandered sweating through the bleak wilds of Highgate West Hill for a street called Holly Lodge

---

[70] 'Guildhall School, On the Level', *The Stage*, 14 December 1950.
[71] 'The Southwellian', vol 6.2, p21; 'The Southwellian', vol 6.5, p38.
[72] 'Southwell Topics... The New Gilbert & Sullivan?', *Newark Advertiser,* 20 February 1952.
[73] *Angus Mackay Diaries*, 3 July 1952.

Gardens. Of course the house I wanted was at the top of the topmost hill; when I arrived in none too good a temper, but prepared to apologise for being about a quarter of an hour late, I was made furious by finding that Donald C. and girlfriends were still en deshabille, and no one else had yet turned up! Oh dear!'[74]

It's an intriguing glimpse of Cotton's life at this time. *The Stage* reviewed the 27 June presentation of *Pandarus*, giving us a sketch of the play's plot and a few hints of its style:

'The opera is a burlesque of the period immediately before the siege of Troy. Pandarus, the court magician, later compelled to become the court undertaker, is responsible for various love-potions, which induce young men, mostly princes, to fall for the somewhat solid charms of his niece Cressida.'

The review commends the play as being 'full of delightful humour'[75] while taking some issues with the staging that may reflect Angus Mackay's concerns when he got involved with a potential professional remount in 1952[76]. What's very clear is the play deliberately exploited anachronism for comic effect. Paris wears period costume but carries a modern portmanteau suitcase and Helen enters as 'the American leader of a chorus of glamour girls'[77].

---

[74] *Angus Mackay Diaries*, 6 July 1952.
[75] 'Guildhall School *Pandarus*', *The Stage*, 5 July 1951.
[76] I can find no record of the piece being restaged, beyond mention of 'a provincial try-out' prior to professional production in *The Newark Advertiser*, 20 February 1952.
[77] *The Newark Advertiser*, 20 February 1952.

This kind of juxtaposition of ancient and modern is something we'll become familiar with in Cotton's later work.

It's around this point that Donald Cotton met Donald Tosh's sister[78], who Cotton later claimed he'd been engaged to[79], though Cotton's wife Hilary Wright has queried this memory[80]. It's possible the joke told about Donald being 'the most engaging man around town' may have some bearing on this difference of opinion. Tosh, having trained at LAMDA, was acting at the time and according to Cotton, he recommended Tosh for a role in a try-out of a play at the Irving Theatre which Cotton couldn't take on himself[81].

Tosh remembered being immediately impressed by Cotton: 'We both got on like a house on fire, because he was very, very, clever and very and very witty. He had a wonderful way of playing with words'[82]. Tosh was not the only one to be impressed by his friend's learned wit. Cotton's colleague June Dixon remembered him as 'the product of an upper-class education' in her memoirs and Nigel Robinson, his later editor at Target Books, described him as 'one of the most erudite men I've ever met.'[83]

---

[78] Evans, Andrew, 'Script Editing **Who**: Donald Tosh', DWM #191, p11.
[79] Tosh in *Myth Makers #44*, Cotton in *Myth Makers #79*.
[80] I suspect incorrectly assuming Cotton was claiming to have been engaged to her at the time of writing *The Myth Makers* (Testro, *Myth Maker* episode 2).
[81] 'Donald Tosh, Story Editor on **Doctor Who** During the William Hartnell Era: Obituary'; *Myth Makers* #44; Walker, Stephen James, ed, *Talkback: The Sixties*, p117.
[82] 'Script Editing **Who** – Donald Tosh', p11.
[83] Testro, *Myth Maker* episode 1.

Wine, Women and Song

After his time at the Guildhall School, Cotton began to specialise in intimate revue[84], performing in and writing for a series of shows primarily for Donald Monat. Joining him in Monat's company was Tony Snell, who later recalled that he and Cotton 'sometimes shared the stage, their accommodations and the occasional struggling actress' during this period[85].

Cotton's work at this time took in comic monologues, song lyrics and parodies of figures as diverse as Sherlock Holmes, the Sitwells, AA Milne, Rudyard Kipling and Nöel Coward, with Cotton dropping aphorisms about the actual price of 'free love'[86]. The Monat productions seem to have offered quite a sophisticated and rarefied flavour of revue, with one reviewer commenting 'the satire, though abundant in wit, is too mild'[87]. Despite this, a song intended for *Light Fantastic,* the second Monat revue to feature Cotton, was controversially rejected by the Lord Chamberlain's Office due to a

---

[84] Intimate revue was a peculiarly British subspecies of variety show featuring song and dance, sketches and monologues that developed in the earlier part of the 20th century. More genteel and literary than music hall, it was usually staged in small theatres as 'after dinner' theatre. (See Moore, James Ross, *An Intimate Understanding: The Rise of British Musical Revue 1890-1920.*)

[85] Sleeve notes, Tony Snell, *Englishman Abroad* (2004), a CD reissue of *Medieval and Latter Day Lays* (1973).

[86] 'At the Theatre, This Word-Play Was Terrific', *Kensington Post*, 18 March 1955; 'Fortune's Smiles Are Many', *The Stage*, 23 June 1955. A version of Cotton's Coward spoof *Private Dives* had been previously performed in *On the Level* for the Guildhall. A re-recording features in episode 1 of Lucas Testro's *Myth Maker*.

[87] Parsons, Ian, 'London Revues 1950 – 1954'.

perceived disrespect shown towards the politicians Winston Churchill and Anthony Eden[88].

A small sample of the type of material Cotton was writing at this time can be found in the short film *Five Guineas a Week* (1956), a compilation of Monat revue items intended to be screened as a supporting feature in cinemas. While the film features the work of several authors and a great deal of straight song and dance, one number, presented in a mock troubadour style, is definitely Cotton's work – a song featuring a mildly amusing lyric about a knight regularly called upon to perform acts of derring-do which result in him gaining the hand of innumerable maidens[89].

Cotton wrote further pseudo-medieval material, perhaps reflecting a love of history recalled by Hilary Wright[90]. There are, for example, three 'lute songs' commended by *The Stage* in *Airs and Graces*, his revue for the Irving Theatre with musical collaborators Brian Burke and Alan Langford. The review also claims Cotton 'has rescued intimate revue from the rut into which better-known authors have lately condemned it', with the slight caveat that 'he plays rather insistently on his own rather macabre note, but some of the items are so original that this slight monopoly is easily forgiven.'[91]

Airs and Graces was a new revue Cotton wrote away from Monat's

---

[88] 'Great Britain, Always the Bridesmaid', *Time*, 23 August 1954.
[89] The number, identified as 'The Lute Song' in the 'Visual Bonus Features' PDF accompanying *Myth Maker* reappears, slightly reworked as 'Hired Knight's Day' on Tony Snell's album, *Medieval and Latter Day Lays* (1973).
[90] Testro, *Myth Maker*, episode 2.
[91] 'Witty Irving Review', *The Stage*, 10 March 1955.

company to showcase Phillipa Reid, who he considered his muse. Cotton had become smitten with his co-star in *Light Fantastic*, who The Stage declared had made 'a grimly diverting thing of' Cotton's 'Caligula', 'a witty, macabre love-song'[92], that one assumes had Classical undertones. The relationship appears not to have lasted long and the pair never collaborated again after *Airs and Graces*.

Several items of Cotton's mock-timbered period comedy were later recorded by Tony Snell on *Medieval and Latter Day Lays*, intoned by Snell in the manner of a slightly more debauched Michael Flanders. The first of these, 'The Lay of the Last Crusader' relates a knight's attempts to prevent his love being untrue while he's away crusading. The second, 'Gypsomania', portrays a country baron bent on the amorous pursuit of a young traveller. The third, 'Ball at Hall', depicts an aging rural roué, 'a gift horse who's constantly kicked in the teeth' ruing his diminishing success exercising his 'droit de seigneur' in his rusticated pile[93].

The song's crusty central character doesn't seem too far removed from the persona Cotton was beginning to cultivate in public to disguise his underlying shyness. Dressing in the tweeds that became his signature style and increasingly affecting the manner of a squire from the sticks, he was to become a regular fixture at the Soho

---

[92] '*Light Fantastic*, Revue at the King's, Hammersmith', *The Stage*, 29 June 1954.
[93] Further examples of Cotton's more macabre side can be found on Tony Snell's album: 'Fungus', a celebration of the joys of dankly rotting away and 'Brownie', in which a country gent recounts a series of murders he's committed.

drinking club, The Kismet, where his aphoristic wit was celebrated[94]. In his biographical sleeve notes for Tony Snell's album, Cotton wrote that he 'lives quietly in the country, and noisily in town', which feels very much in keeping with the image he hoped to project. His noisy living appeared to include quite a lot of alcohol.

Cotton's writing also led to television work toward the end of 1958 with credits on three episodes of **Better Late!** (1958), a BBC series attempting to capture the feel of late-night revue on screen, and a co-writing credit on *The Merry Christmas*, a musical adaptation of *A Christmas Carol* with revue colleague Brian Burke, broadcast on Christmas Eve by Associated-Rediffusion.

The Demon Barber, a short-lived musical about Sweeney Todd[95], again co-written with Burke, followed in late 1959, but drew poor notices[96]. The play was described as 'a glum piece of would-be comic

---

[94] Artist and British TV personality Giles Wood writes in passing on page 127 of *The Diary of Two Nobodies* of his:
> 'wicked uncle Donald Cotton's dodgy antiquated Norfolk jacket, which he used to wear around the drinking dens of Soho, such as the Kismet Club, in order to build up the mystique of himself as a countryman and as if in denial that he was in the Metropolis.'

Cotton was a friend of Giles Wood's mother, Ann Wood, rather than a blood relation.

[95] *The Demon Barber* ran from 10 December 1959 to 9 January 1960 at the Lyric Theatre, Hammersmith.

[96] *The Stage* described it as 'a feeble adaptation', 'the blood and thunder gone and replaced by burlesque which flies wide of its mark.' ('Two Sweeney Todds: RB Marriott on the Musical', *The Stage*, 17 December 1959).

macabre' by JC Trewin in *The Illustrated London News*[97], who in a further review for *The Birmingham Post* bemoaned its running time of nearly three hours and described some of Cotton's rhymes as 'adventurous', citing 'knew that the hot-head would cut his carotid' as an example. My guess, given the subject matter and Cotton's style, is that he will have been going for a triple rhyme here, combining 'hot-head', 'carotid' and 'garrotted'.[98]

A Happy Medium

Meanwhile, Cotton had found a new outlet for his work, enjoying a fruitful collaboration with BBC radio producer Douglas Cleverdon. Between 1959 and 1965, Cleverdon and Cotton collaborated on nine projects for the BBC's Third Programme.

Cleverdon employed Cotton as a writer, as the host of a miscellany of spoken and sung word[99], and twice as an actor[100], on Third Programme projects.

Four of Cotton's plays with Cleverdon were pieces satirically placing modern day concerns in Classical or historic trappings. The first, *Echo and Narcissus* (1959), plays with genetics through the prism of Greek myth, featuring a Narcissus, who, mistakenly believing his father to have been Zeus in swan form, thinks he has a unique chromosomal

---

[97] Trewin, JC, 'The World of the Theatre, A Pair of Villains,' *Illustrated London News*, 26 December 1959.
[98] Trewin, JC, 'The Demon Barber at Hammersmith', *The Birmingham Daily Post*, 12 December 1959.
[99] *Voices in the Air* (1960).
[100] Cotton plays DH Lawrence for Cleverdon in *A Dialogue on Pacifism* (1964). The casting could easily have been influenced by an ability to do a Nottinghamshire accent.

structure which means he's incapable of loving the nymph Echo. The second play, *The Salvation of Faust* (1960), presents psychiatry as a snare of the devil[101]. The third, *The Golden Fleece* (1962), described to *The Stage* as 'a modern version of the Euridice story, set in a road-house called The Golden Fleece'[102] features figures from Greek myth alongside a reporter played by Cotton himself. The fourth, *The Tragedy of Phaethon* (1965), deals with the son of the sun god Helios and his paradoxical discovery that the gods do not in fact exist.

In a short introduction to the play for the *Radio Times*, Cotton disregarded *The Golden Fleece*, describing the other three works as thematically linked:

> '*Phaethon* is the concluding play of a trilogy begun in 1959 with *Echo and Narcissus*, and continued in 1960 with *The Salvation of Faust*. All three plays are concerned with the problems confronting the enthusiast who becomes a fanatic. In *Echo* the target was genetics applied to marriage guidance; in *Faust* it was psychiatry considered as a universal panacea; in *Phaethon* it is youth's rebellion against convention.'[103]

The Tragedy of Phaethon is full of Cotton's trademark wordplay, with the goddess Venus bemoaning the 'incessant incest' of Olympus and advising Phaethon in song against opposing his father with the lines:

> 'Frankly, you're the feebler. An enfant terrible

---

[101] 'Look and Listen', *Uxbridge and West Drayton Advertiser and Gazette*, 30 June 1960. Cotton had previously written and narrated a short piece entitled *The Salvation of Faust* which he presented on stage in 1952. This may well be an earlier version of the radio piece.
[102] 'To Play Euridice', *The Stage*, 19 April 1962.
[103] BBC Genome Radio Times listing, 'The Tragedy of Phaethon.'

Is not yet an éminence grise.'

A neat example of Cotton's 'adventurous' rhyming, coupled with a show of verbal dexterity as he slips into borrowed French. The play is essentially comic, dropping esoteric allusions into casual chat and, on one occasion, giving a hint of the ghoulish undercurrents sometimes detected in Cotton's writing:

CLYMENE

Really, Phaethon, women twist you around their fingers! Let me tell you about Venus...

PHAETHON

Yes, you have done several times.

CLYMENE

She is no better than she should be. Had to change her name from Aphrodite, not that it fooled anybody for a moment. She was born in what I can only call the most disgusting circumstances imaginable. Your uncle Chronos happened to be mutilating your grandfather Uranus with a sickle at the time, so, of course, we were in a position to know.

This exchange is both mythologically accurate and, like a lot of myth, pretty grotesque if examined closely.

It's tempting to project elements of Cotton's personal background onto the play. Phaethon is a free-thinking youth in love with music, Venus and the pursuit of knowledge. His parents are a fussing, doting mother and a distant, essentially missing father who disapprove of and attempt to thwart his rebellious individualism. If his family life did inform the piece, there's a certain sadness in the fate of Cotton's hero – doomed to orbit erratically around his parents rather than ever escape their pull.

The play also features some mild satire aimed at politicians, forced like Olympian gods to make personal appearances to prove they exist, and presents its clash of the Titans and Olympian gods in the language of the Cold War, with each side monitoring Phaethon's movement remotely and communicating by radio. Ultimately, beyond its jokes, it centres on the conflict of established religious tradition and rationalism, something which we'll also see in *The Myth Makers* in the tension between Achilles and Odysseus.

The Tragedy of Phaethon and *The Myth Makers* came about at a time when the wider culture had conveniently fallen into step with Cotton's classically bent wit. In 1964 *A Funny Thing Happened on the Way to the Forum*, a witty musical farce based on the work of Roman playwright Plautus, had been a hit on the British stage and the **Carry On** film producers had felt moved to spoof the Hollywood epic *Cleopatra* (1963) in *Carry On Cleo*. The influence of both comedies had already been felt on **Doctor Who**, which had presented its own Classical farce *The Romans* later in 1964[104]. The appointment of Donald Cotton's old friend Donald Tosh as **Doctor Who**'s story editor meant there was now both an open door and potential TV audience for the kind of thing Cotton had been doing for years.

The translation between mediums was not quite as smooth as we might imagine. Cotton's success in radio and slight fogeyish elitism meant he was unfamiliar with **Doctor Who**. He was not a huge fan of

---

[104] Dennis Spooner's story was later adapted by Donald Cotton for the 1987 Target novelisation as a series of fictional documents compiled by the ancient historian Tacitus.

television, and was initially unsure how to approach writing for it[105]. Additionally, Cotton's radio plays have less than we might imagine in common with his TV scripts beyond dealing comically with legendary figures. They play with 'breaking the fourth wall', acknowledging their own fictional status, a device **Doctor Who** has very rarely dared deploy, slipping into verse and occasionally song[106], and happily blend epic and vernacular and ancient and modern. *The Myth Makers* is stolidly naturalistic in comparison, and the closest it comes to replicating this gleeful anachronism and inconsistency of tone is in its use of language – placing puns in the mouths of ancient Greeks and Trojans that can only function in modern English and bathetically juxtaposing high-flown poetic speech with conversational dialogue:

PRIAM

(TO THE OTHERS)

Come my children, our people have gone to the square of Oratory, and I must speak to them. Afterwards we'll have to discuss the plans for the celebration.

(BACK TO VICKI)

See you later my dear, and thank you.

The actor Max Adrian, who played Priam, had appeared in five of Cotton's plays, and, according to Lucas Testro, was a longstanding

---

[105] Recalled by Hilary Wright, in Testro, *Myth Maker,* episode 2.
[106] *The Gunfighters* is arguably closer to Cotton's radio work, thanks to introducing sung narration in 'The Ballad of the OK Corral' and deploying the series' first fourth-wall-troubling 'Doctor who?' joke.

friend of Cotton[107]. This seems to be borne out by Donald Tosh's recollection of Cotton telephoning Adrian to ask him to play Priam in *The Myth Makers*[108].

Adrian was an esteemed and witty performer who had famously been jailed for homosexual importuning in 1940, and his sexuality is believed to have made William Hartnell uncomfortable with him during rehearsals[109]. This has been widely reported, though Peter Purves' recollection of the frostiness between the performers makes a general disdain harder to sustain. Purves has Adrian ask him '"Peter, what is the matter with Bill? He won't speak to me, and I've known him for years." It was baffling to him,'[110] which doesn't suggest a long-standing enmity. Donald Tosh suspected Hartnell's insecurity in the face of experienced stage actors in the series may also have had some bearing:

> '[O]ld thespians that they all were, rather sent up the local cast. [...] He saw it as a sort of threat, suddenly here were stars that were bigger than him, and Max was wicked, a very funny man, who could suddenly drop in a remark, or deliberately make a mistake, which would then just crease everybody up.'[111]

Hartnell's standoffishness with Adrian has also been ascribed to

---

[107] Testro, *Myth Maker,* episode 2.

[108] 'Script Editing Who', p11.

[109] Purves, Peter, *Here's One I Wrote Earlier*, p97.

[110] Purves, *Here's One I Wrote Earlier*, p97.

[111] Stevens, 'Donald Tosh Interview'. Where Tosh refers to the guests sending up the regulars in the plural he's probably also thinking of Francis de Wolff.

57

personal jealousy and anti-Semitism[112]. It is however worth recording that I've found nothing confirming Adrian was Jewish beyond writings on **Doctor Who**[113].

The Myth Makers' composer Humphrey Searle, probably came to the TV series by a similar route of personal recommendation. He'd regularly collaborated with BBC producer Douglas Cleverdon since composing music for the poet David Gascoyne's piece *Night Thoughts* in 1955, and through Cleverdon had come to write music for three of Cotton's plays.

Searle worked in a number of styles, composing in a conventional western mode, using Schoenberg's 12-tone technique and working in musique concrète using manipulated recorded sound. Searle was a good fit for *The Myth Makers*, having a passion for the Greek classics that had developed at school and Oxford University. In 1959, a visit to the site of Mycenae had inspired the first movement of his third symphony[114] and he composed several pieces touching on ancient Greek themes across his career, notably the music for the 1960 Royal Shakespeare Company production of *Troilus and Cressida* in which Max Adrian had played Pandarus to enthusiastic

---

[112] 'Maureen O'Brien in Conversation', *Doctor Who: The Collection, Season 2*, 2022; Carney, Jessica, *Who's There?*, pp171-72.

[113] Adrian himself claimed to be Anglo-Catholic ('He Was Joky and Hairy and Bony', *The Australian Woman's Weekly*, 22 May 1968). It's possible he was assumed to be Jewish following his 1962 portrayal of Fagin for the BBC. One can, of course, still be the victim of anti-Semitic prejudice if incorrectly identified as Jewish.

[114] Searle's unpublished memoirs have been made available online. Donald Cotton is mentioned, though *The Myth Makers* is not. See Searle, Humphrey, 'Quadrille with a Raven', Chapter 13 'Interlude'.

notices. In later years Searle also composed the music for **The Serpent Son** (1979), Frederic Raphael and Kenneth McLeish's adaptation of *The Oresteia* of Aeschylus for the BBC[115].

While Searle's orchestral and choral work on that series is a world away from the 13 minutes and two seconds of music for eight musicians he supplied for **Doctor Who**, there's a certain musical continuity in the way both evoke a Homeric era through bold stabs of brass.

Despite *The Myth Makers* having gone down well enough with the **Doctor Who** production team to ensure a repeat engagement, things began to turn a little sour for Cotton in the years that followed. His next **Doctor Who** commission was inherited by a new production team which was less enthused with his style and the finished show, *The Gunfighters*[116], went down badly with audiences and BBC TV Head of Drama Sydney Newman[117].

His work on the pilot of the new BBC series **Adam Adamant Lives!** (1966-67) was also poorly received within the BBC, with Cotton's

---

[115] *The Oresteia* relates the tragic events following Agamemnon's return from Troy. **The Serpent Son** (1979) adapted the plays, under the titles *Agamemnon, Grave Gifts* and *Furies*. In his memoir, Searle's particularly praises the series' female cast, which includes Maureen O'Brien as Elektra.

[116] *The Gunfighters'* Audience Appreciation Index figures dropped from 45% to 30% over its four week run.

[117] Newman's memo criticising the serial is quoted in Howe, Stammers and Walker, *Doctor Who: The Handbook – The First Doctor*, p127.

work almost entirely removed on transmission[118]. His confidence was seriously knocked and his work in radio was about to dry up too. The Third Programme was to become Radio 3 in 1967, a station with far less room for Cotton's particular brand of smart silly, and his champion Douglas Cleverdon would retire from the BBC in 1969.

On top of that his marriage was breaking up. In 1964, Cotton had married Hilary Wright, an actress he'd met while she was working as a barmaid at the Kismet Club, and though they now had a young son, things were not going smoothly. Cotton was living chaotically, perpetually either flush with cash from a freelance commission or utterly broke, drinking heavily and becoming as emotionally absent a father as his own had been to him. At his impromptu wedding reception, naturally held in a pub with an audience of strangers, he'd quipped 'Ladies and gentlemen, I feel like a person who's just won the pools. And like anybody who wins the pools says, it will not alter the way I live one bit.' He seems to have been true to his word[119].

Back to the Boards

Despite the flop of *The Demon Barber*, Cotton had continued to work in theatre in the early 1960s, returning to his native Nottingham and contributing to the Nottingham Playhouse revues, *Second Post* (1961) and *Yer What?* (1962) as well as premiering a new piece of musical theatre there in 1961.

---

[118] **Adam Adamant Lives!** is generally considered Sydney Newman's brainchild and Newman's dissatisfaction with both *The Gunfighters* and Cotton's contribution to **Adam Adamant Lives!** probably put an end to further television drama work for the corporation.
[119] Testro, 'Man Out of Time', p25.

Mam'zelle Nitouche was an adaptation of 19th-century French comic opera in which an apparently pious music teacher at a convent school led a double life as a songwriter in the unrespectable world of musical theatre. With music by James Stevens, who'd worked with Cotton on the Third Programme, the piece had been updated by Cotton to produce an audience-pleasing farce[120].

Cotton would revive *Mam'zelle Nitouche* at the Connaught Playhouse in 1969 and the Pitlochry Festival in 1971, in both cases playing the role of Fernand. *The Stage* review of the Pitlochry revival praised the play, recommending it to 'the lover of words and wit' for its 'dialogue and lyrics of bright originality and at times Gilbertian oddity'. The review also described Cotton as 'superbly roaring and bloodshot as the lustful General Major Ferdand'[121]. Cotton would increasingly specialise in larger-than-life characters like Fernand, offering several permutations on his eccentric country gent in plays across the country over the next decade.

In 1969 Cotton and Stevens went deeper into 'Gibertian oddity' with *My Dear Gilbert*, a musical play exploring the working relationship of Gilbert and Sullivan alongside extracts from their work. Jon Pertwee, soon to be announced as the new lead in **Doctor Who**, played the lead role of Gilbert, but of more significance to Cotton in the cast was the singer Eileen Shaw, who was to become his new partner[122].

Cotton enjoyed a fruitful collaboration with the Connaught Theatre

---

[120] 'Chorus Girls from Convent', *The Stage*, 13 April 1961.
[121] 'Mam'zelle Nitouche', *The Stage*, 13 May 1971.
[122] Cotton's *Daily Telegraph* obituary ('Playwright, Actor Had Wide Range of Talents', 28 January 2000) describes her as his second wife but there's no evidence the relationship was formalised.

in Worthing from 1969 to the mid-1970s, with the theatre offering him numerous roles[123] and staging revivals of *Mam'zelle Notouche, My Dear Gilbert* and *The Demon Barber*. Reports he nearly decapitated the actor David Beale with a prop axe while rehearsing *A Man for All Seasons* there in 1974 appear to be exaggerated[124].

The late 1970s saw Cotton regularly working with the Northampton Repertory Theatre company at the Royal Theatre, Northampton, acting with the company in a number of productions between 1978 and 1980 and showing the first signs of new writing in years with his new comedy, *Love Between Friends*. Eric Shorter, writing in the quarterly magazine *Drama*, praised Eleanor Bron's central performance, adding that:

> 'Mr Cotton contrived some good epigrams for her in this comedy of platonic platitudes and Miss Bron put them all to fine sardonic use as a middle-aged spinster who plighted her celibate love for a boy in her school days and has kept her word ever since. He has been less continent but their mutual affection has never waned and the comedy describes various threats to their celibate bliss.'[125]

---

[123] Roles included Sir Hector in *Thark*, Sir Peter Teazle in *School for Scandal*, Benbow in Brahms and Sherrin's *Benbow was his Name*, Redfern in *Look Back in Anger*, pantomime roles in 1970 and 1971 and The Common Man in *A Man for all Seasons*.

[124] The story related on p17 of *The Book of Luvvies* appears to be another tale that has grown in the telling. In *The Stage*'s account, the blow hit Beale's head and only six stitches were required. 'On This Week at... Worthing', *The Stage*, 2 May 1974.

[125] Shorter, Eric, 'Plays in Performance, Regions', *The Quarterly Theatre Review*, Summer 1976, p71.

The play was considered to have West End potential by *The Stage*, which described it as 'witty' and noted that it 'ends on a wistful note-almost a sigh of pathos.'[126]

Cotton went on to write more for Northampton, a new historically based comedy *The Ballad of Mrs Beeton* in 1978, the pantomime *Dick Whittington* and an adaptation of *Wuthering Heights*, and appears to have formed a platonic bond of his own with a young actress during his time at Northampton, taking the teenager Tamsin Wickling (to whom he dedicates his novelisation of *The Gunfighters*) under his wing[127]. The man who charmed Tamsin does not seem to have been the lusty country gent Cotton had played so successfully for decades, but a more kindly presence keen to educate the young woman[128].

Cotton seems to have retired from acting 'with relief' in 1981[129]. He apparently continued writing plays, but the only visible theatrical activity beyond this point is a pair of restagings of *The Demon Barber* by The Bristol Old Vic Theatre School in 1985 and 1996[130].

It was around this time that **Doctor Who** reappeared in Donald Cotton's life after almost two decades estrangement.

---

[126] 'Love Between Friends', *The Stage*, 18 March 1976.

[127] In Testro, *Myth Maker* episode 3, actor Nicholas Lumley remembers Cotton being 'madly in love' with Wickling, though she interprets their relationship differently.

[128] Testro, 'Man Out of Time', p27.

[129] Walker, *Talkback: The Sixties*, p117.

[130] In 1985 apparently retitled *Sweeney Todd, The Demon Barber of Fleet Street*, perhaps with an eye to enticing fans of the similarly titled Sondheim musical from 1979.

Novel Departures

By the mid-1980s, Target Books' series of **Doctor Who** novelisations had moved on from being a conveyor belt of titles, usually adapted by Terrance Dicks, aimed at younger readers. The readership was now a little older and stories from earlier in the programme's history were being adapted, with the original authors increasingly being approached to rework their scripts. Donald Cotton novelised *The Myth Makers*, *The Gunfighters* and Dennis Spooner's *The Romans* between 1985 and 1987, adopting a style which allowed him to apply his colourful narrative voice far more freely than more conventional Target novelists.

Cotton's devotion to puns, literary references, colourful phraseology, brazen anachronism and the natural world shines through in all three works, as does his chosen comic persona. The narrators that frame these works, Homer, Ned Buntline and Tacitus, are all chatty, digressive writers concerned with book sales, theatrical fame and payment, much as Cotton presented himself in his printed recollections of **Doctor Who**[131]. The novels radically restructure the television serials, partly reflecting the source material Cotton had to hand, partly to accommodate his new narrators and, more than anything, in hot pursuit of jokes.

In Toby Hadoke's extended interview for *Myth Maker: The Lost Legacy of Donald Cotton*, he observes that Cotton will happily take liberties with the portrayal of the Doctor for the sake of a gag in these novels, and this is, in fact, characteristic of Cotton's overall approach. If there's the potential for wordplay, a pun, or comical

---

[131] Walker, *Talkback: The Sixties*, pp116-18.

image he's happy to enable it, even if it's occasionally at the expense of clarity or unlikely to land with his target audience. He'll meander for half a page to make a joke about the river Meander. Despite *The Myth Makers* being stripped of the Olympian gods, he'll allude to Helen's divine origin story just to furnish a fun detail. His Homer knows French and Latin (let's not worry immediately about his English) and paraphrases Shakespeare. He makes reference to the Flying Dutchman, Rodin's The Thinker, Pythagoras, Damascus steel, possums, raccoons, boa constrictors and budgerigars. He confuses chronology more than Virgil did in sending Aeneas to Carthage[132], by having Homer and a middle-aged Vicki and Troilus present at the burning of the Library of Alexandria[133]. It's a *1066 and All That* approach to the ancient world, containing 'all the parts you can remember'[134], and Cotton's Homer is a modern, if occasionally old-fashioned, man, adrift in a time of myth. The effect is delightful, if occasionally distressing to that literal-minded part of all **Doctor Who** fans that still vainly wants it to make proper sense.

Cotton wrote one more novel for Target in 1986, *The Bodkin Papers*, a children's book that emerged from conversation with Target editor Nigel Robinson over a boozy lunch. The book, intended as the first of a series, related the adventures of an extremely loquacious parrot who'd witnessed some of history's greatest moments and was now

---

[132] If there was a historical Dido of Carthage, her reign would have dated to around the eighth century BCE, centuries after the Trojan War.
[133] The burning of the Library of Alexandria occurs around 48BCE.
[134] WC Sellar and RJ Yeatman's book *1066 and All That* (1930) was a comic history of Britain built around often misremembered famous moments.

dictating his memoirs. The book initially seems to be launching a variant on Michael Bond's Paddington, but quickly moves on from the children Josiah meets in the present to offer another of Cotton's digressive and unreliable accounts of history as the parrot explains its role in the development of Charles Darwin's theory of natural selection, returning to the theme we encounter in *The Tragedy of Phaethon* of the conflict between religion and rationality. Cotton's playful prose is in evidence throughout:

> 'Moving with the alternative apathy and energy of perigee and apogee, the moon began the long haul from its tree silhouette-infested nadir to a zenith where it hoped there'd be rather more room for it.'[135]

The book's essential problem is it's aimed at children yet written with no real concession given to a child's tastes, understanding of idioms or general level of literacy. It occasionally uses racial terms one might have expected a 1980s publisher to flag as inappropriate and returns to jokes about drink and broken marriages a few times too often. It's all a bit too silly for adults and a bit too sophisticated for children, never quite escaping the uncertainty of who it's aimed at. Nigel Robinson left Target Books in 1987 and the projected sequel featuring Josiah and Rasputin failed to materialise[136].

---

[135] Cotton, Donald, *The Bodkin Papers*, p31.
[136] At DWASocial 5, Cotton expressed a desire to write a third Bodkin book about Karl Marx. It's hard to imagine the books being a playground hit.

Final Days

After Cotton's work with Target dried up, he moved back to the Hastings area where he'd once lived with Hilary Wright and began work on a novel Tamsin Wickling recalls being a melancholy affair about an old man reflecting on his life.

Cotton appears to have sold off a few items relating to his **Doctor Who** work at auction in 1996 and died in hospital on 29 December 1999. He'd developed a lung infection and pneumonia after being badly injured falling backwards downstairs. The coroner's presumption was the accident occurred while Cotton was drunk[137].

---

[137] Testro, *Myth Maker* episode 3.

CHAPTER 4: THE UNRAVELLING TEXTS

'So, having commissioned Donald to write *The Myth Makers*, I was then presented with a four volume novel. The scripts were literally inches thick, and, as television, would have ran for 90 minutes each. They were brilliant. They were wonderful, but oh, god, it was a nightmare cutting them down into 25-minute episodes.'

[Donald Tosh, 2011][138]

'I can't quite recall why the script ended up as jokey as it did. That was probably the Donald Tosh influence since "jokey" was one of his favourite themes. I would probably have liked to have made it more serious but at the time I was more interested in testing the temperature of the water to see what we could do, and how far we could take the format.

[John Wiles, 1983][139]

As befits a serial built on the back of fragmentary documents, frustratingly brief synopses, and multiple evolving retellings, *The Myth Makers* survives in several partial iterations that warrant close scrutiny. Treating these texts[140] as archaeological evidence, we can attempt to glean some idea of the author's original intent, track the serial's development, examine production decisions that refined it, and draw comparisons with the author's approach when

---

[138] Stevens, 'Donald Tosh Interview'.
[139] Bentham, J Jeremy, 'John Wiles Interview', *DWM Winter Special 1983*, p9.
[140] Here I'm treating the audio record of transmission as a 'text' existing between camera script and novelisation.

reinterpreting his material in novel form. When examining early storylines and draft scripts I'll focus chiefly on how they differ from the final scripts and the synopsis presented at the start of this book. Discussion of the camera scripts and transmitted episodes will also take in production trivia and cut lines where identifiable, and attempt to highlight and explicate some obscure references and jokes.

For simplicity, I'll be looking at the development of each episode in turn.

'Deus Ex Machina' – Written Breakdown

One reason fandom has tended to treat the Troilus and Cressida subplot as a late addition to the serial is access to what was always believed to be Donald Cotton's first storyline, a typewritten scene breakdown which drifts markedly from the transmitted story as it progresses and makes no mention of Troilus or Vicki's renaming. However, recently uncovered texts reveal additional stages of development that allow us to look at this storyline in a new light. It's now clear that what we believed was Cotton's first scene breakdown actually represented second thoughts and that much of the serial's plot was in flux from the beginning. The texts in question are a series of handwritten scene breakdowns and script drafts preserved in a notebook inherited by Donald Cotton's son[141].

Cotton's *Myth Makers* scene breakdown begins with a proposed list of characters in which Steven is referred to as Michael[142]. The character list continues with various Greek and Trojan figures, most

---

[141] Testro, Lucas, 'Troy, Troy, Troy Again', DWM #581, pp29-31.
[142] 'Mike' in the scene descriptions that follow.

of whom will appear in the final serial. Some names, however, have a cross placed by the side of them, suggesting Cotton has second thoughts about using them, and two are entirely scribbled out. The names with crosses by their side are all women of Troy – 'Helen', 'Hecuba' and 'Andromache'. One of the two scribbled-out names is 'Cassandra'. A second, which is slightly harder to make out, is almost certainly 'Homer'[143].

This scribble suggests Cotton considered and dismissed featuring Homer in the production very early on. We can only speculate what role Cotton might have had in mind for him. Perhaps a conventional narrator, or a bard recording events with a suggestion his tale would grow in the telling? It's possible Cotton might even have toyed with something akin to the role Homer fills in his 1985 novelisation. All we can be sure of is that he quickly thought better of it.

The scene breakdown for episode 1, at this point titled 'Deus Ex Machina'[144], opens on Hector pursuing Achilles on 'the plains of Scamander before the Trojan walls', taunting him for having

---

[143] The image in the digital edition of DWM is not high resolution, but the name can be made out if zoomed in on.

[144] 'Deus ex machina', literally meaning 'god from the machine', is a Latin term for a practice in Classical Greek theatre, in which a mechanism (probably involving a winch and pulley) was used to have a god descend to the stage and put straight the problems of mortals at a drama's end. It's from this that the phrase's modern use, meaning a contrivance designed to reconcile a plot, arises. The Doctor offers us both kinds of deus ex machina in Cotton's storyline – he emerges from his machine appearing to be Zeus and essentially pulls a resolution to 10 years of war from nowhere.

withdrawn from the war[145].

Scene 2 has Odysseus, Menelaus and Agamemnon observing the heroes on the plain from the Greek camp, wishing they'd start fighting rather than indulging in 'schoolboy rhetoric'[146]. Agamemnon's true reason for waging war (to 'control the trade routes to the Black Sea') is established here.

Scene 3 sees Priam, Paris and Helen observing the heroes' combat from Troy's walls, indulging in 'pointed back-chat' criticising Paris. The additional character names Hecuba and Andromache are dropped in above the line, though their markings on the preceding cast list suggest Cotton quickly decided against their inclusion[147].

In scene 4 Achilles declares he's invincible due to being backed by Zeus, unlike the Trojans who are supported only by Aphrodite[148]. Hector demands Zeus descend if this is the case and then falls to his knees as 'Tardis materialises behind Achilles and DR. Who emerges' as if on cue. Taking advantage, Achilles kills Hector and 'The DR.

---

[145] This is an inversion of Achilles' pursuit of Hector during their final battle in The Iliad that will pay off later when the scene breakdown is expanded to script.

[146] A wink to the depiction of battle in The Iliad, which routinely involves lengthy pronouncements by the heroes both as a prelude to and punctuation of combat. This is apparent throughout The Iliad, but is particularly notable in the confrontation of Hector and Achilles parodied here (The Iliad XXII pp403-06 in the Rieu translation).

[147] Cotton may have been unconsciously influenced by memories of the play X=0 in the structuring of these opening scenes. The action of Drinkwater's play takes place in a tent in the Greek camp, on top of the walls of Troy and briefly on the plain between them.

[148] Respectively the father of the gods and the goddess of love.

remonstrates slightly'. Cotton adds an afterthought in the margin here – '(2 scenes of reaction in Greek camp and Troy?)'. Achilles takes the Doctor to be Zeus, and in a delightfully idiosyncratic note Cotton writes 'DR Who realises he has arrived in time to assist a victory with which he has always been out of sympathy and is somewhat peeved.'

In Scene 5 we discover Mike has witnessed but not fully followed this action on the 'scanners'[149]. Telling Vicki to stay behind he goes out to investigate.

Scene 6 has the Doctor claim the TARDIS is a portable temple and introduce Mike to Achilles as the god Mars[150]. Achilles begs the gods to come to the Greek camp with him, and the Doctor agrees, unable to resist this chance to meet the heroes.

In Scene 7, Menelaus and Agamemnon revere the travellers, but Odysseus remains suspicious of them and gets Achilles to take him to the TARDIS to examine it. Mike follows them.

Scene 8 was initially set in 'A hall in Priam's palace' but this has been scribbled out in favour of a scene on the Trojan plain. Paris and a group of Trojans have headed out to recover Hector's body, and discover the TARDIS. While dragging it off to Troy they're ambushed by Odysseus and Achilles. In the ensuing conflict Paris shoots Achilles in the heel with an arrow. Mike arrives and helps Odysseus get

---

[149] This reference to the TARDIS having scanners in the plural is an idiosyncrasy of Cotton's that survives into the finished programme and its novelisation. The only other onscreen mention of the TARDIS having more than a singular scanner occurs in episode 1 of *The Curse of Peladon* (1972).

[150] Technically this should be Ares. Mars is the Roman name.

Achilles away but he's been fatally wounded. Odysseus begs Mike to use his power as the god Mars to save Achilles' life, but Mike can do nothing. Learning Mike is a time-traveller, Odysseus promises to keep this secret in exchange for help securing Troy's fall.

In Scene 9, responding to the loss of Achilles, Agamemnon vows to mount a final assault on Troy. Concerned for Vicki and the TARDIS, the Doctor proposes the idea of the Trojan Horse to Odysseus.

A remarkable amount of this first episode outline makes its way to the finished script. The sparring of Achilles and Hector and the arrival of the TARDIS seem almost entirely fully formed. Much of the scene between Agamemnon and Menelaus quoted in Chapter 1 draws on scene 2 proposed here, and The Doctor's treatment as a god, Odysseus' scepticism and the TARDIS being taken to Troy with Vicki still aboard it are all broadly in place. What's more remarkable is all the additional action proposed and the rate at which plot is chewed up. We are introduced to several Trojan leads an episode earlier than on TV, and Achilles is slain (as tradition dictates by an arrow shot by Paris[151]) three episodes earlier than in the final scripts[152]. Most strikingly of all, we're straight into the Doctor proposing the Trojan Horse by the end of episode 1.

The Doctor's enthusiastic desire to meet the Greek heroes and his

---

[151] The story of Achilles' being invulnerable to injury bar on his heel thanks to being dipped in the river Styx as a baby isn't referred to in Homer. In fact *The Iliad* has Achilles suffering several injuries.

[152] As transmitted, Achilles' heel finally proves his comeuppance when he catches it in some vegetation in 'Horse of Destruction' and dies at the hands of Troilus. This is another reversal of traditional fortune for the Trojan prince new to *The Myth Makers*.

active engagement in shaping history both feel a little out of character here, as does his only mild remonstration at the death of Hector. It's also notable that the series' nominal leads seem to have a bit less to do than the guest cast, with Vicki in particular contributing almost nothing to the story.

Additionally, there are some suggestions of Cotton's background in radio and the possibility he may be vamping his story as he goes here. His lack of consistency over whether or not the site of the duel of Achilles and Hector and the TARDIS' arrival can be seen from the Greek camp and Trojan city suggests he's not fully visualised the story, and his use of abutting scenes featuring performers in new locations, following a lapse of time, is much more characteristic of radio storytelling than 1960s TV[153].

'Deus Ex Machina' – Typed Breakdown

By the time of the typed-up scene breakdown retained by the BBC, episode 1 has undergone a few changes. The action has been streamlined and focused and the supporting Trojan cast has dwindled to Hector alone.

Scene 1 still sets up Hector and Achilles, but the TARDIS arrives more quickly. Scene 2 now has the Doctor Mike and Vicki observing them.

Scene 3 has the heroes fight around the TARDIS not registering it as

---

[153] With the use of recording breaks and videotape editing, this kind of narrative approach was achievable on **Doctor Who** by 1965 and, while several time lapses of this nature occur in *The Myth Makers*, it's not typical of British TV at the time, which, broadly speaking, had established an 'as live' visual grammar based on earlier technical limitations.

out of place. It is now the Doctor emerging that provides the distraction which allows Achilles to slay Hector[154]. Achilles still takes the Doctor to be Zeus, but now high-spirited Greeks whisk him and Achilles away to camp despite the Doctor's protestations. While this loses the impact of the ship materialising to Hector's amazement, the Doctor's being delivered to the Greek camp seems more plausibly engineered.

Scene 4 sees Mike go in pursuit much as he had in the previous storyline's scene 5. It is followed by a scene marked '(telecine?)' which sees him sneak into the Greek camp. Lucas Testro points out that the technical detail here is atypical of Cotton and may suggest Tosh had a hand in this revision.

Scene 6 recaps the Doctor being treated like a god in a tent at the Greek camp but without the inclusion of Mike as Mars. Odysseus remains sceptical and goes outside [155]. He sends a spy into Troy and

---

[154] This change may have been made to avoid the technical challenge of having the TARDIS arrive in the middle of live action.

[155] Odysseus is misspelled 'Oddyseyus' at one point here, one of several misspellings of the name across the document, perhaps evidence of someone typing at speed. Testro suggests this might be further evidence of Tosh's hand at work, though several misspellings of 'Vicki' suggest the typist may have been someone less familiar with the series. Whoever typed out this scene breakdown, it's probably the fiddly spelling of the name Odysseus that increasingly leads to it being abbreviated to 'Od.' Or 'Odd.' as the document progresses.

discovers Mike.[156]

Odysseus' use of spies is introduced here, despite Cotton later claiming his spy character, Cyclops, was devised during the rewriting of episode 3. Odysseus being tied to spying fits with his depiction in Book X of *The Iliad*, in which he and Diomedes spy on Thracian allies of Troy and manage to capture a spy of their own.

Scenes 7 to 9 are proposed here as a series of cross cuts (possibly another sign of Tosh interceding). Across these, Mike tells Odysseus he and the Doctor are not gods, the Doctor persuades the Greeks to let him recover the TARDIS, and Vicki feels the TARDIS jolt and knocks against its controls.

Scene 10 has Mike and Odysseus arrive at the TARDIS' landing spot to find it gone. Mike thinks it may have dematerialised with Vicki on board, and the cross cut sequence feels contrived to give viewers the same impression.

This version of the plot is now very close to the televised episode, and, while it still short-changes Vicki, it serves the regulars better. However, there's an intermediary text between this scene breakdown and the camera script. Cotton's notebook also provides us with handwritten scripts for *The Myth Makers'* first two episodes, which I've been kindly allowed to access.

---

[156] One other quirk of this text that may help point us toward its author is some occasionally arbitrary capitalisation, including the routine rendering of Greek gods as 'Gods'. This seems to rule out the document being typed by Cotton, whose handwritten scripts all spell 'god' and 'gods' in lower case.

'Deus Ex Machina' – Written Draft

This handwritten script follows the typed storyline fairly closely and much of it closely resembles the final camera script but there are several striking differences and details.

The opening sequence is imagined very cinematically, something we had no real sense of in the synopses, with Cotton clearly picturing this action being filmed on location[157]. In Hector's first line, he mockingly calls out to Achilles, using the form of his name favoured by some classicists, 'Achille-u-s...!' The desired effect would seem to be similar to someone crying 'Yoo-hoo!' or 'Coo-ee!' Confusingly in this draft, while the character is always referred to in stage directions and speech headers as Achilles, he's referred to as Achilleus throughout the dialogue, with the Doctor reasoning this is an early form of the name which comes down to us as Achilles. This notion and the related dialogue will be dropped in the camera script which changes Hector's cry to a more straightforward 'Achilles...!'

Achilles responds to Hector's taunting by calling Hector a 'horse-master!' It's just possible given Cotton's propensity for wordplay, literary allusion and mild innuendo, that he hoped this to be taken,

---

[157] The sequence is indeed filmed on location and Cotton's handwritten stage directions detailing his proposed shooting are retained in the camera script, though as this was a document primarily intended for studio use that doesn't guarantee they were followed. However, the recollections of long-term fan and fellow **Black Archive** author Dene October strongly suggest Cotton's ideas were broadly followed (Robson, Eddie, 'Eye Witnesses: *The Myth Makers*', DWM #568, p25).

if only fleetingly, for the Shakespearean insult 'whore-master'[158]. The line is expanded on in the final script, with this specific taunt replaced.

Hector's description of Achilles as a 'light-foot princeling' is a fair summation of the legendarily fleet-footed hero[159]. Cotton may, however, have had a secondary sense of light-footedness from British slang in mind, where it has been used to impute effeminacy.

The exchange in which Achilles and Hector describe Patroclus as a boy suggests a slight departure from Homer, who has both Achilles and Patroclus as youths with Patroclus the slight elder. The dialogue is also slightly trimmed in its final scripted form[160].

The references to offering bones to dogs and leaving them to whiten in the sun may allude to Achilles' threat in *The Iliad* to leave Hector's body on the battlefield for dogs and carrion birds, and his later pledge to Patroclus' shade that he'll leave it 'for the dogs to eat it raw'[161].

Scene 2 opens with the Doctor remarking that he's returned the

---

[158] The phrase occurs in *Troilus and Cressida* as 'whore-masterly' and is used in four other Shakespeare plays.
[159] In the Rieu translation of *The Iliad*, Achilles is called 'Achilles of the nimble feet' during his fight with Hector (*The Iliad* XXII, p404).
[160] The novelisation reinstates the longer version of this dialogue as featured here, right down to Cotton's use of 'loth', a less common spelling of 'loath' (Cotton, *The Myth Makers*, p16). This is not the only time unaired material from this draft is reinstated in the book. It seems Cotton had access to either this manuscript or an unknown later draft based on it when composing the novel.
[161] See *The Iliad* XXII p406 and *The Iliad* XXIII p412 in the Rieu translation.

travellers to Earth, and a late addition to the line suggests he was trying to get Mike home. The Doctor believes they're in prehistoric times and misidentifies their location as probably being the Kalahari, receiving sarcastic praise from Mike. There is some discussion of the area as being one of the cradles of civilisation, before the Doctor embarks on a factually accurate description of the Bush Men of the Kalahari, marred only by the suggestion of them possibly coexisting with dinosaurs. It's likely, given Cotton's interest in natural history, that he's deliberately playing up the Doctor's dufferish incompetence here. Cotton's unfamiliarity with **Doctor Who** is made clear here through mention of the TARDIS air-lock[162].

A few pages of proposed line changes follow the handwritten scripts in Cotton's notebook. Amended lines for this scene now refer to Mike as 'Steven', and feature the Doctor stating that where they've landed is better than where the Doctor found him. These notes appear to be for an unknown version of the script, because the page numbers given for proposed line changes don't tally with those in either the notebook or final camera script.

Scene 3 has one notable passage of dialogue between Hector and Achilles which is lost in the later camera script but partially restored in Cotton's novelisation:

HECTOR

Run, Achilleus, run! Show me your heels! Run just a little more, before you die!

---

[162] No other televised **Doctor Who** script has included a reference to the TARDIS air-lock, although it does feature in a couple of *TV Comic* stories postdating *The Myth Makers*.

What – don't you want to leave a legend? Wouldn't you like the poets to sing of you, eh? Not even 'swiftest of the Greeks'? Must I rob you of such small distinction?

ACHILLES

Hector, by all the gods, I swear.....

HECTOR

The gods? What gods? Do you so much as dare to swear by your petty pantheology? That rag-bag of squabbling, hobbledehoy Olympians? Those little gods to frighten children? Ha! 'Do be good or Zeus will get you!' 'Do get up, Apollo's rising!' What sort of gods are those?[163]

It's an exchange that sets up two of the story's major themes – the rejection of gods and how men become myths.

Scene 5, Achilles' first meeting with the Doctor, is slightly longer than it ends up on screen, and it's during this exchange that the Doctor realises 'Achilleus' is an early form of the name Achilles. When the Doctor realises Achilles has killed Hector, he gives an aside that sheds light on Cotton's attitude to the Doctor changing history.

DR. WHO (Half to himself)

Dear me, so that's how it happened. I could never understand

---

[163] Transcribed from Cotton's notebook. The novelisation's reworked version appears on pages 16 and 17. 'Swiftest of the Greeks' is a common English rendering of one of Homer's stock descriptions of Achilles. It does not appear in Rieu's version of *The Iliad*, despite regular references to Achilles' swiftness, as Rieu studiously avoids describing the various Greek forces as Greeks.

the outcome of this particular battle! So it was my fault all the time... I really must be more careful...[164]

These lines will not survive in the camera script and the Doctor will not be noticeably more careful as the story continues.

The business of Achilles kicking Hector's corpse, the Doctor protesting that one mustn't kick a man when he's down and Achilles prostrating himself is additional material again detailed later in the notebook. The Doctor's dialogue is slightly lengthier than on screen, including the phrases 'bless my soul' and 'Good heavens', which may have been intended to position him as religious or ease his identification with a deity. What is notably missing is the Doctor's shock at Hector being dead.

In the previous encounters Achilles describes featuring Zeus in disguise, that of Europa with the bull and Leda with the swan[165], Zeus takes on those forms in order to have sex with a human. Achilles was either being very forward or failing to fully think things through, when comparing these liaisons to his meeting with Zeus. It's only in this version of the text that Cotton spells the joke out:

DR. WHO

Well, in this case, you see, my motives in descending are somewhat different from the previous occasions to which

---

[164] Transcribed from Cotton's notebook.
[165] In some tellings of her story, Helen of Troy is Leda's daughter, born from an egg as a result of her mother's union with the swan Zeus. Cotton also alludes to Leda and the swan in *Echo and Narcissus* and the novelisation of *The Myth Makers*, when he incongruously addresses Helen's apparently divine origins (p82).

you refer.[166]

Speeches reinforcing Menelaus' excessive drinking and the importance of minstrels singing songs in one's honour follow Achilles' demand that the Doctor comes to the Greek camp. These are removed in the camera script[167]. Significantly, this sequence is the first to establish the Trojans have 'pagan horse-gods'.

The scene, as first written, continues directly to the arrival of Odysseus, and his line about having cut a number of Trojan throats is slightly more gruesome than in the final version.

ODYSSEUS

A half score Trojans will not whistle easily tonight. We found 'em laughing by the ramparts; now they smile with their bellies.[168]

In Cotton's later notes, he appends the short scene of Steven and Vicki watching the action from the TARDIS that will split this lengthy sequence and appear in the camera script as scene 10.

One small but regrettable tweak to the script is Odysseus' observation that the TARDIS is perhaps Zeus' 'week-end temple'. I suspect literal-minded readers queried this anachronistic phrase[169].

Scene 6 is a fairly lengthy discussion between Vicki and Mike in the

---

[166] Transcribed from Cotton's notebook.
[167] The broad sweep of the exchange is replicated on page 23 of Cotton's novelisation.
[168] This kindly cut is reversed on p25 of the novelisation.
[169] The weekend is a development of the industrial age, dating from either the mid-18th or early 19th century depending on precisely how you define it.

TARDIS in which they establish they are not in the Kalahari. Mike makes an impressive logical leap from the Greek costumes, their arrival on a plain and the sight of a mud-walled town on a hill to intuit they've arrived during the Trojan War. The broad thrust of this is retained in Chapter 7 of Cotton's novelisation. The scene ends with mention of both the 'scanners' and 'air-lock' as Vicki wonders what 'Agamemnon really is like.......'[170] to lead us into the next scene.

Scene 7 is broadly the camera script's scenes 13 and 15 in Agamemnon's tent, though here the action is continuous. This version features a handful of expanded lines between Agamemnon and Menelaus. Odysseus' cutting description of the Doctor here as 'this old dotard' will be softened to 'this old man' by the time of transmission. A small trim is also made to Agamemnon's questioning of the Doctor in the camera script, but this section broadly follows Cotton's handwritten amendments to this scene. Shortly before Odysseus leaves the tent, Cotton proposes an insert revealing Mike approaching the tent, presumably realising his imminent discovery needs to be set up. Odysseus' withdrawal is slightly more bad-tempered in this draft than it ultimately becomes, with him asking permission to go to his tent where the air is free of the other Greeks' 'credulous sanctity', itself a substitution for a crossed out 'cloying superstition'. Odysseus is more circumspect on transmission.

The scene's final exchanges are somewhat simplified in later drafts. As presented here, the Doctor claims Agamemnon cannot kill him but attempting to may cost him the war. Agamemnon then debates what to do with Menelaus, who is too nervous to make a hard and

---

[170] Extended ellipsis is Cotton's own.

fast judgement over whether the Doctor is a spy or divine.

As a compromise it is decided to place the Doctor 'under a form of very reverend arrest'. In a pointed passage dropped from the camera script but largely retained in the novelisation[171], Agamemnon describes this as 'a probationary period of cautious worship,' adding 'You mustn't be offended. After all, most gods are, to some extent, the prisoners of their congregations.'

Scene 8 sees Mike captured by Odysseus outside Agamemnon's tent. This closely resembles the conclusion of scene in the camera script but concludes with a slightly more poetic flourish, with Odysseus comparing Mike to a moth attracted to the camp's light and inviting him to singe his wings as he throws him into Agamemnon's tent. However, in his additional notes that follow the handwritten scripts, Cotton adds a new opening to the scene in which 'Cyclops', the mute one-eyed spy of Odysseus, warns him Steven is approaching in sign language. This seems at first glance to put paid to Cotton's claim that this character was a late imposition dropped into his existing scripts[172]. However, Cotton's story may still carry a grain of mythologised truth.

Odysseus having a spy present in this scene was a notion introduced

---

[171] Cotton, *The Myth Makers*, p41.

[172] Walker, *Talkback: The Sixties*, pp117-18. In brief, Cotton claims Cyclops arose because his proposed title for episode 3 was rejected. An alternative title, 'Death of a Spy', was suggested, which Cotton queried, pointing out the episode contained no spy and was now fully scripted, with no space for to additional more lines. Cotton states this then led to the introduction of a mute spy who would require no additional dialogue before meeting his end.

in this episode's typed scene breakdown, and the character's lack of speech makes a certain amount of sense if we imagine he is in danger of being captured and spilling secrets in the line of his work. However, Cyclops does feel a surprisingly visual character for a writer who rejoices so much in language. It's just possible the mute Cyclops was proposed by Donald Tosh as a device to avoid some of the lengthy dialogue scenes Cotton leant towards.

Having been made mute, the character would then need to be easily identified by viewers as he moves between the Greek camp and Troy. This might in turn have led to his being made one-eyed and have inspired the 'Cyclops' nickname. Cotton's claim that Cyclops was forced on him, and his reworking of the character in his novelisation of *The Myth Makers*, suggests the character was an aspect of the story Cotton remained unhappy with[173]. Cotton's post-script notes also rework the scene ending into something much closer to the camera script, losing the moth imagery but gaining Odysseus' scornful description of the Doctor as 'a hungry god' at Agamemnon's table. Sadly, a further description of him as a 'decrepit trickster' doesn't make it through.

Scene 8 is very close to what appears on screen, with just a few short trims. It does, however, end before the appearance of Cyclops in Cotton's first pass. The original ending has the Greeks agreeing to go to the TARDIS tomorrow, to witness the Doctor's miracle.

We then cut to scenes 9 and 10, in which Vicki nervously watches

---

[173] In the novelisation, Cyclops' role is largely given to Homer, allowing the book's narrator to take an active part in the plot. The happy accident of the one-eyed Cyclops becoming the legendarily blind poet, is one of the book's most pleasing innovations.

Trojans approaching 'Tardis' on 'the scanners' before being thrown to the ground as the ship jolts. Outside we see it being dragged away to Troy. Cyclops' sequence is again an addition from later in the notebook.

An additional script for this episode is likely to exist in private hands. A Bonhams catalogue listing a number of Cotton's **Doctor Who** items sold at auction in 1996 offers the following description:

> 'A collection of original manuscripts, typed scripts and draft novels from the Donald Cotton collection, including "Mythmakers", "Gunfighters", "Romans", "Small Prophet Quick Return", "Heroes Of Destruction", "Dues Ex Machina", some typed, others handwritten, all signed. Estimate £400 – 500.'[174]

These items for auction clearly include scripts for three episodes of *The Myth Makers*. Perhaps the most tantalising inclusion here is one for what has to be 'Horse of Destruction'. This may be, as 'Dues Ex Machina' [sic] certainly must be, another version predating the surviving camera script.

'Temple of Secrets' – Script and Screen

On transmission, the episode title 'Deus Ex Machina' has finally given way to the more prosaic 'Temple of Secrets'. This is one of several Cotton title substitutions Donald Tosh put down to producer John

---

[174] Ricks, Steven, 'Bonhams Flashback...'

Wiles' desire not to feature anything 'jokey'[175].

In scene 1, the camera script replaces Achilles opening taunt of 'horse-master', expanding the line to 'stable-keeper, barbarian, horse-worshipper!' This immediately establishes the serial's rationalisation for the Trojans' willingness to accept the Wooden Horse. We will in time learn that the Trojans worship 'The Great Horse of Asia', rather than the Greek pantheon as usually imagined[176].

This is an invention of *The Myth Makers*, with no clear precedent in either tradition or the archaeological record. Horses do however feature prominently in Mycenaean art, making the Greeks far more likely horse worshippers of horses[177].

The opening of scene 2 in the previous draft (labelled in the camera

---

[175] 'Script Editing Doctor Who', p11. Cotton returns to his more playful original for his novelisation, refining it to 'Zeus Ex Machina' as the title of Chapter 2. The extra layer of wordplay is facilitated by the words 'deus' and 'Zeus' having derived from the same root.

[176] One possible spur to Cotton's imagination in devising the Great Horse of Asia may have been his reading of NGL Hammond's *A History of Greece to 322 BC* while researching for *The Myth Makers*. On p53 Hammond makes passing mention of the Trojans having introduced the horse to Asia.

[177] There is in fact a prominent Greek god of horses – Poseidon, a deity who had a diverse portfolio of interests despite being primarily known to us as a sea god. Poseidon actively supports the Greeks in *The Iliad*, though he occasionally takes pains not to be seen to do so and sometimes intercedes disguised in the form of an old man. In a version of *The Myth Makers* truer to *The Iliad*, it's Poseidon the Doctor would have been taken for.

script as scene 4)[178] has been removed in this final version, though a line with Steven reacting to the Doctor's presumption they are in the Kalahari is retained (feeling like a slight non sequitur now it's shed of context). The joke at Homer's expense about the heroes talking more than fighting that appears in the first scene breakdown has now been placed in the Doctor's mouth. Vicki's relegation to the TARDIS interior in this episode is now justified in this script by reference to an ankle injury incurred at the end of *Galaxy 4* (1965). This injury is mentioned in a late script change to *Galaxy 4*'s final scene that was almost certainly introduced to rationalise Vicki's reduced involvement in 'Temple of Secrets'[179].

The topic of Steven's sarcasm (now largely cut) is raised at the scene's end. The intent seems to be a sort of comic bathos, suggesting the sword-wielding combatants outside might not take kindly to Steven's mild brusqueness. However, in performance Hartnell delivers the line as 'your kind of sarcasm'. Given sarcasm derives from the Greek 'sarkazein' (literally 'to cut flesh'), it could conceivably be argued that Hartnell's attempting to sell a fairly esoteric gag here about different ways to be cutting. I don't consider

---

[178] I can't account for the discrepancy in scene numbering here. My best suggestion is that this scene inherits the number 4 from earlier abandoned plans. Scene 1 is entirely shot on film, but the intention may have previously been that it should begin on film, move to studio for the dialogue portion and then return to film as fighting commenced, giving three scenes. This is, however, pure conjecture.
[179] Ironically, the discussion of Vicki's ankle replaces dialogue in which she pines for a more settled life, which might have helped foreshadow her departure if it had been more carefully planned.

it likely, but it's possible[180].

The scene in the camera script has been slightly tightened throughout since the manuscript, and its rewriting throws up a curio which allows us to identify other pages which may have been reworked. The Doctor is listed here as '**DOCTOR:**' as opposed to '**DOCTOR WHO:**', which appears on almost all other pages[181].

In the 1960s, any changes to a script for wider distribution would have to be made manually. Most cuts would be handled by blanking out sections of text, occasionally retyping small sections of dialogue over the blank section to ensure the lines still made sense with the edits. To reduce the labour involved, only pages that required considerable work would be fully retyped, and we occasionally see evidence of this in format changes like this.

One slight production inconsistency emerges here: much of the action inside the TARDIS in this episode depends on the time-travellers being unable to hear what's going on outside and so failing to understand what they see. Despite this, dialogue between Hector and Achilles can be heard in the background of this scene. A sequence in the handwritten scene breakdown for the next episode seems to rely on dialogue spoken outside being audible within the

---

[180] As we've seen, abstruse and esoteric jokes are a characteristic of Cotton's writing even when writing children's fiction. In *Myth Maker* episode 3 Nicholas Lumley recalls an obscure Classical joke Cotton scripted for the *Dick Whittington* pantomime at Northampton, which raised one solitary laugh across the play's run.

[181] This is probably Tosh's preferred form, faithfully recorded by a BBC typist.

TARDIS, which makes this inconsistency stand out more[182].

The opening of scene 5 has been streamlined slightly since Cotton's notebook draft, losing about half of Achilles' and Hector's opening speeches. Similarly, Hector's dying words are cut from two sentences to one. Hector's scripted description of Achilles as a 'dartdodging decadent'[183] early in the scene might have been considered dramatically ironic if Achilles had gone on to be killed by an arrow, as he is in legend and Cotton's first scene breakdown.

Page 11 of this script again finds '**DOCTOR:**' substituted for '**DOCTOR WHO:**' in the dialogue headers. In both Cotton's notebook and novelisation, this sequence has the Doctor tell Achilles he has to 'get back to the others'. Achilles takes this to mean other gods and the Doctor does not correct him. This was likely a trim for clarity and time. The suggestion the Doctor has companions in his 'temple' is redundant now Steven is not to be mistaken for Mars.

At the end of scene 6 it's unclear why Steven feels he should change into period appropriate clothing when the Doctor has not. It's possible he suspects the Doctor's outfit has contributed to his getting mixed up in things, but this is never articulated.

Scene 7, which precedes a brief model shot of Troy noted as scene 8, retains a short section of Achilles' speech mentioning Trojan minstrels from the notebook draft, in which he states the Greeks rot

---

[182] The TARDIS scanner's ability to handle sound varies considerably, dictated by the demands of stories and preferences of production teams. However, the opening episode of *Galaxy 4* has recently established that the scanner can relay audio during this era.

[183] 'dart-dodging' in the handwritten script, a late tweak of 'arrow-dodging'.

in the Trojans' summers and 'starve in their crack-bone winters'.

Scene 9 sees what will become *The Iliad*'s version of the duel of Hector and Achilles begin to take mythical shape. Odysseus mockingly suggests Achilles has chased Hector around the walls of Troy, and Achilles, failing to contradict him, builds up his part, claiming to have defeated Hector through his greater strength after at least an hour in combat. Odysseus' exclamation 'what a year this is for plague!' further implies some factual seed for the plague sent by Apollo to punish the Greeks in *The Iliad*.

This draft introduces a moment of the Doctor protesting at the killing of Hector, which as scripted is barely more vociferous than his slight remonstration in the handwritten scene breakdown. However, Hartnell plays the lines with sufficient angry bluster to make the sequence work. Scene 9 also features a single line on page 16 in which '**DOCTOR WHO:**' once more becomes '**DOCTOR:**', again indicating rewrites. The cut sequence here has Achilles chide Odysseus for his 'blasphemy and laughter at the gods' and explain to 'Zeus' that Odysseus joined their 'holy cause for booty'[184].

In scene 11, Odysseus' suggestion that the Doctor tell 'a tale or two of Aphrodite' over supper may be an obscure allusion to the bard Demodocus presenting a story of Aphrodite that Odysseus hears during a feast held by the Phaeacians in Book VIII of *The Odyssey*[185].

Scene 12 sees Vicki inherit the eagerness to meet the Greek heroes

---

[184] Achilles' speech is retained in the novelisation (p27).
[185] *The Odyssey*, Rieu translation (pp129-132). It's at this same extended banquet that Demodocus later tells the tale of the Wooden Horse.

that was given to the Doctor in Cotton's handwritten storyline. If we had only this final version to go on, we might have charitably interpreted this moment as one meant to foreshadow Vicki's willingness to stay in this time period.

Fan reviewers may have occasionally read too much into Agamemnon's description of Menelaus as a 'dropsical old camp follower' in scene 13[186]. It may sound suspiciously like some form of sexual innuendo is at play here, but dropsy is a form of swelling caused by fluid retention associated with alcoholism, and a camp follower is a term for a non-combatant accompanying an army. On balance, this seems like a fair summation of the drunken Menelaus, although his actor Jack Melford does not appear noticeably bloated in other roles around this time. One thing we do miss by having no pictures of Melford as Menelaus is that he would indeed have looked quite old (he would have been 65 at the time of recording). Casting the slight, elderly Melford as the younger brother of Francis de Wolff's vigorous Agamemnon may have been amusingly incongruous on screen, with Wolff being an imposingly big, dark-haired actor in his 50s. Menelaus' appearance may also help account for Helen's willingness to be abducted by young Paris. When Helen's previous abductions are referred to, the myth of her having been abducted by Theseus in her youth is being invoked.

The account of a cowardly Paris having refused to face Menelaus in a fight that would have settled their dispute, and Agamemnon's

---

[186] Graham Kibble-White includes it in a list of lines featuring the 'posh boys' trick of disguising jokes about base topics in fancy attire' (Kibble-White, Graham, 'Missing in Action: *The Myth Makers*', DWM #496, p73).

dismissal of him as a coward, is a fair extrapolation from Homer. In *The Iliad*, Paris is rescued by the goddess Aphrodite from a disastrous fight against Menelaus[187], and Paris is seen to generally rely on his bow and arrow rather than fight face-to-face as other heroes do[188].

A few lines between Agamemnon and Achilles are very slightly trimmed on pages 27 and 28. The cut material emphasises Agamemnon's lack of respect for Achilles and spells out that he's not averse to using propaganda for military purposes. Some of this is retained on p36 of the novelisation.

Scene 13 sees a slight variation between the script and its realisation. In Cotton's stage directions he suggests serving wenches attend the Greeks[189], but the performers cast here as drinks bearers are a young boy and girl, a change perhaps made in the interests of reflecting the period. The boy, Stephen Ubels, would have been in his teens, and is the son of Doreen Ubels who appears as a Trojan woman in episode 2. The opening of this scene occurs on page 21 of the script, which then instructs the reader to move '**ONTO PAGE 24**', the next numbered page. This indicates a section of the script has become several pages shorter through rewrites around here. The note saves the production the trouble of having subsequent script pages renumbered.

Scene 14 is a film insert which establishes the TARDIS being taken off by the Trojans. The idea of misleading the audience into believing

---

[187] *The Iliad,* Book III, Rieu translation, pp72-74.
[188] In *The Iliad*, Book XI, Rieu translation, Paris shoots Diomedes in the foot from the cover of a distant column and is condemned by the Greek as a coward (p207).
[189] 'Temple of Secrets' camera script, p24.

Vicki has accidentally dematerialised the ship has now been abandoned, although Steven will continue to suspect this at the start of episode 2. The end of this sequence visually reinforces the idea of Trojans as horse worshippers, with the camera dwelling on a plaque bearing an image of the Great Horse of Asia.

Scene 15 sees the Doctor reveal that Clytemnestra, Agamemnon's wife has been unfaithful in his absence. This information presumably comes from knowledge of *The Odyssey* or other later literature dealing with her relationship with Aegisthus, the ruler of Mycenae in Agamemnon's absence[190]. The Doctor then plays on the phrase 'the Glory that was Greece', though placing it here in the present tense. It's a phrase coined by Edgar Allan Poe in the 1845 revision of his poem using Homeric imagery, 'To Helen'.

In the handwritten script the Doctor speaks of the 'might of Greece'. While the Doctor is still some way from proposing the Wooden Horse, he already seems to be blithely introducing the people he's meeting to literary responses to their lives from the future.

Page 29 sees a small whited-out passage and the only capitalised use of God in this script[191], both of which point to rewrites. In the finished script the Doctor asks 'If am not a God, how do you account for my supernatural knowledge?' In the manuscript this is a small-letter god. The rewrite is probably due to cutting a small section of dialogue from the previous draft which didn't drive the plot forward.

Further areas of blank space on page 32 reveal Achilles' opening line

---

[190] Most notably *The Oresteia* play sequence by Aeschylus.
[191] This revised line is the only time 'god' or 'gods' are capitalised in their 11 uses across the 'Temple of Secrets' camera script.

and the Doctor's reply to it have both been trimmed. Versions of the extended dialogue are present in both the notebook manuscript and Cotton's novelisation. Here Achilles expands on his pledge to deal with Odysseus for the Doctor, explicitly offering to kill him. The Doctor dissuades him, stating Odysseus is an able servant of his and will shortly bring about the fall of Troy. The line trim means the Doctor's assumption that Achilles intends to kill Odysseus seems a bit of a mental leap, and it feels a shame to have lost another example of the Doctor imparting future knowledge with this edit[192].

There is an oft-repeated production anecdote relating to the final line of this scene. Francis de Wolff, who Peter Purves recalls had taken a dislike to William Hartnell, is supposed to end the scene inviting the Doctor to sit down and have a ham bone. de Wolff is said to have paraphrased the line as 'sit down ham and have a bone,' presumably as a slight on Hartnell's acting though it could plausibly have been a genuine slip of the tongue[193].

I've always been wary of taking this on trust and have assumed that if it did occur it would have likely been during rehearsals. However, Peter Purves remembers it as having happened during the recording and has stated 'it caused an unscheduled 'Tape Stop' – a real rarity

---

[192] A version of this sequence occurs on p40 of the novelisation. If the Doctor's concern about keeping history on track after causing the death of Hector had been retained in the camera script, it might have gone some way towards justifying how readily he reveals Odysseus' future role in the war. The Doctor is so eager to see Odysseus live to fulfil his literary destiny that he predicts and consequently sets it.

[193] Purves, *Here's One I Wrote Earlier...*, p97.

in **Dr Who**. But the bad line had to be expunged.'[194]

Scene 17 introduces Cyclops, as discussed in the manuscript version of this sequence. Curiously, in the one picture of Cyclops' actor, Tutte Lemkow, in costume, both his eyes are just visible, with no evidence of any eyepatch or special make up that might have indicated partial sightedness.

Although the notebook manuscript and this camera script both refer to Cyclops as one-eyed (in identical stage directions) they give no indication at all of how this was realised in studio[195].

Scene 18 gives us the cliffhanger of the TARDIS having vanished, introduced in the typed scene breakdown, now slightly weakened by simply being reported.

The episode ends with a shot of the Trojan plaque we saw near the TARDIS in scene 14, making clear that the empty bit of plain we're

---

[194] Quotation from direct message chat with the author, 20 April, 2023. Purves has previously remembered the incident as occurring during rehearsals (Marson, Richard, 'Interview: Peter Purves', DWM #121, p8).

[195] Lemkow had previously played a character with a patch over his left eye in the **Doctor Who** story *Marco Polo*, which I suspect may have conditioned us to expect the same of Cyclops. As Lemkow's left eye is the one almost obscured in *The Myth Makers'* image we might tentatively suggest it was also the one covered in performance and that this photo was framed hoping to disguise a patch's absence. Cyclops is definitely said to wear a patch on the narration read by Peter Purves for *The Myth Makers* audio release in 2001 and the fact none of the programme's surviving fan viewers seem to have queried this strongly suggests he did. Frustratingly, Peter Purves recalls Lemkov's appearance during rehearsals but not during recording (direct message chat with the author, 20 April 2023).

looking at is one where we previously saw the TARDIS. This may have been a flourish introduced by the director, Michael Leeston-Smith, most of whose **Z Cars** (1962-78) episodes end on a close up of a significant item or a now empty location from earlier in the episode[196].

Episode 2 – Written Breakdown

The handwritten scene breakdown for the untitled episode 2 opens with a fresh list of characters. Three of those listed, Hecuba, Helen and Andromache, will not appear in the episode's final form[197].

Scene 1 opens in a marketplace, later amended to a public square, in Troy. Paris and a group of Trojans have dragged the TARDIS there. Paris informs Priam and Hecuba of the death of Achilles, and it's decided to ceremonially burn the TARDIS, which the Trojans have seen was instrumental in the death of Hector.

Scene 2 finds Vicki in the TARDIS, watching the fire being prepared, initially unperturbed, but deciding to emerge after Cassandra fails to persuade Andromache and Hecuba that destroying the TARDIS would insult the gods. At this point it seems Cotton imagines Vicki

---

[196] This is apparent even in the two episodes that survive only as Tele-snaps (*The Hitch-Hiker* and *Members Only*). The only exception to the rule is *Tuesday Afternoon*, which ends on a photograph of three of the guest cast.
[197] Cotton doggedly attempting to include this group of female characters leads me wonder whether he might have planned to riff on their appearance in Euripides' *The Trojan Women* at some point. *The Myth Makers,* as originally conceived, extended some way beyond the fall of Troy and the post-war fates of Cassandra, Hecuba, Helen and Andromache are central to Euripides' play.

can hear what's being said outside the ship.

In scene 3 Vicki is hailed by Cassandra as a messenger from Olympus. In square brackets Cotton toys with identifying her as Aphrodite, but asks 'How old is Vicki?' a question we'll return to later. The Trojans hail her as a saviour. There are a couple of points of interest here. Cotton has clearly not yet fully committed to the notion of Cassandra always being ignored, presumably limiting this characteristic to her prophecies at this point. Secondly, we can see that he is still treating the Trojans as sharing the Olympian gods with the Greeks, having not yet devised his Great Horse of Asia.

Scene 4 opens on the walls of Troy the next day. The Greeks have apparently sailed away, leaving the Wooden Horse behind. Vicki is credited with saving the city and Priam orders that the Horse be brought into the city. Cassandra predicts disaster but Vicki contradicts her, having realised Troy needs to fall if she's to rejoin Mike and the Doctor[198]. The shift to the next day is slightly problematic here, suggesting the Wooden Horse plan has gone from its proposal to completion overnight.

Scene 5 covers the Horse being dragged into Troy and scene 6 reveals the Doctor, Mike, Odysseus and a number of Greek soldiers are within it.

Scene 7 sees another transition to night, as the Greeks, the Doctor

---

[198] In some ways the loss of the Trojan walls location in the final programme is regrettable. Foregrounded actors on the wall with a model set behind could have been very effective in integrating the Horse and human action. Unfortunately, the location raises more problems than it solves with regard to what the enemies can and can't see of each other's activities.

and Mike leave the Horse. The Greeks slay the Horse's Trojan guards and open the city gates to the rest of the Greek forces.

A stray fragment of an attempt to write up this part of the story line in script form may survive in the one remaining page of a run of pages ripped from Cotton's notebook. The extract in full reads:

after himself......

Scene 19. The gates of Troy.

AGAMEMNON (hammering on gates):

Odysseus, where in Hades are you?

ODYSSEUS (above):

Here, commander.

AGAMEMNON:

About time, too[199]

Mike and the Doctor go to the TARDIS only to find Vicki missing. Cotton considers having Odysseus examine the TARDIS here but decides against it.

Scene 8 involves the Greeks and Trojans fighting, and scene 9 involves the death of all the Trojan heroes bar Aeneas who is reported to have escaped; in square brackets Cotton imagines there will be words about this from the Doctor. Priam is killed with arrows

---

[199] There's obviously also an argument in favour of this being a passage from a lost version of episode 4. There isn't quite enough evidence to make a judgement either way.

as Agamemnon enter his palace[200]. Paris dies at the hands of Menelaus, who takes back Helen in the process[201]. One does not get the impression Cotton has yet pictured Menelaus as the bibulous old coward that Jack Melford will play. The Greeks divide the spoils of war among themselves, Agamemnon claiming all the women of Troy and Odysseus the TARDIS. This fairly brutal sequence of events brings us to a cliffhanger that reminds us how much of the story of the Trojan War comes down to men claiming ownership of women.

As it stands, this scene breakdown offers Vicki a lot more to do than episode 1, but in summary form it leaves her open to accusations of cruelty, as she seemingly accepts the destruction of Troy as a price worth paying if she's to rejoin her friends. There is, however, much less action for the Doctor and Mike, with the story focusing on its secondary characters facing each other in battle, and the whole episode seems seriously short of incident when compared to episode 1's equivalent breakdown.

Episode 2 – Typed Breakdown

The story resumes with Odysseus getting Mike to hide with him as the Greeks bring the Doctor to the plain. With the TARDIS gone, the Doctor has no miracle to offer and, no longer considered a god, he is

---

[200] Priam's traditional death at the hands of Neoptolemus, son of Achilles, is somewhat nastier, particularly in the artistic depictions that have him being beaten to death with the corpse of his infant grandson.
[201] This tidies up the fussier tradition in which Paris is killed by another Greek, Philoctes, before the fall of Troy and Helen is passed on to Paris' brother Deiphobus who is subsequently slain by Menelaus in most accounts.

taken back to camp as a prisoner. Odysseus stays behind with Mike, curious, as the document puts it, about 'this strange stranger'.

Scene 2 finds the TARDIS in the main Trojan square as in the previous scene breakdown and the Trojans grieve Hector as before, but Andromache and Hecuba are no longer mentioned. Cassandra now warns that the TARDIS is full of Greek soldiers and demands its destruction. As Priam asks the gods for a sign that'll make clear whether the TARDIS can be trusted, Vicki emerges.

In scene 3, we learn Odysseus' spy has witnessed these events as he reports them to Mike and Odysseus. Odysseus agrees to help Mike get Vicki back, disguising him as a peddler so he can enter Troy[202]. Odysseus also engineers a meeting between Mike and the imprisoned Doctor. Mike explains about Vicki, and the Doctor fills in Mike on the fall of Troy. Odysseus' help is conditional on the Doctor engineering an end to the siege within 48 hours.

There's no scene 4 listed, but Mike's meeting with the Doctor would have presumably taken place in it. Scene 5 finds Mike and Odysseus' spy getting into Troy, where Mike is unfortunately detected and captured.

Scene 6 features Vicki at Priam's palace, struggling to play the role of a divine messenger in the face of Cassandra's scepticism, when Mike is brought in by guards. Vicki gives away her recognition of Mike and, challenging Vicki's authority, Cassandra orders that Mike

---

[202] Odysseus has both a history and future with disguise which Cotton may be alluding to here. The goddess Athena disguises him as an old beggar on his return home in *The Odyssey*, and there is a post-Homeric tradition of him having recruited Achilles to the Trojan War through a subterfuge involving dressing as a peddler.

be put to death.

The scene breakdown ends here, feeling some distance short of 25 minutes of incident. It does, however, broadly follow the scripted episode's eventual plot. The Doctor's role here is very much reduced, but that is not entirely uncommon during this run of **Doctor Who**[203], and the finished episode will feature him in just three scenes.

'Small Prophet, Quick Return' – Handwritten Draft

By the time it reaches Donald Cotton's handwritten draft, episode 2 has been gifted with a jokey title too good to be rejected by its producer[204]. 'Small profit, quick return' idiomatically refers to pricing items low to sell them in large numbers. This piece of advice to retailers was also referred to by the initials SPQR, with the phrase possibly being a back formation devised to fit them (the letters would already been familiar in popular culture as standing for the Roman motto 'Senatus Populusque Romanus', and the abbreviation would often be seen on Eagle standards in representations of Roman legions). Cotton's punning play on the phrase is so fitting I suspect the quick returning part of the episode[205] may have been deliberately engineered to justify it.

---

[203] The Doctor has a much reduced role in *The Massacre* and barely features in episode 11 of *The Daleks' Master Plan* or episodes 2 and 3 of *The Celestial Toymaker* (all 1966).

[204] Tosh remembered this being the only one of Cotton's more playful of episode titles he won the battle to retain. 'Scripting Editing Who', p11.

[205] The flitting of Cyclops from Troy to the plain and back.

Cotton's handwritten script again begins with a cast list[206], this time featuring no rejected characters. Agamemnon is a late addition with a question mark by his name who is then moved further up the list with a tick by his name and arrow to indicate he should sit directly beneath the regular characters. It would seem Cotton wrote these lists out before starting work writing the episodes and is now trying to limit cast numbers, probably with an eye to the show's available budget. Cyclops does not feature here.

Scene 1 is indicated to be a recap of the end of episode 1. Scene 2 finds the Doctor, Agamemnon and Mike on the Trojan plain searching for the lost TARDIS. An Odysseus line to the Doctor here has him suggest '…perhaps the weight of centuries has made you absent-minded.' The line works as well for the Doctor as it does for Zeus, but does not make it to screen. Cotton also provided a rationalisation for Achilles not being with them, with Odysseus claiming 'Achilles lies abed. No doubt he felt he'd championed a lost cause, and held it tactful to be absent.'[207] This too will be cut.

Oddly, Odysseus refers to the imprisoned Doctor and Mike as 'mannikins' in this scene. The word is missing from the camera script but is still used by Odysseus on broadcast and in Cotton's novelisation[208].

---

[206] 'DR. Who, Mike, Vicki, Odysseus, Cassandra, Paris, Priam, Agamemnon.'

[207] The idea of calling him Achilleus in dialogue already seems to have been abandoned.

[208] Cotton, The Myth Makers, p50. The word is perhaps cut from the script due to it being of 16th-century Dutch origin, though Salter appears to have already committed it to memory.

The end of the scene finds Odysseus more openly contemptuous of his Greek allies than he will be on screen, calling Agamemnon 'that fool' and offering an equally contemptuous dismissal of Achilles.

ODYSSEUS

[...] That muscle-bound, body-building Narcissus fears his shadow in the sunshine; will not so much as comb his hair until he reads the new day's auguries. He is so god-fearing that he sees gods everywhere – and trembles at them all. [...]

Interestingly, in Cotton's post-script notes he writes 'Do not insert suggested alteration' for 'page 3' of episode 2, which is likely to be this scene. This suggests these notes were made in response to editorial comments on delivered drafts and that, in this instance, he may be pushing back against them.

In scene 3, the TARDIS is dragged into the Trojan square and Paris, Priam and Cassandra squabble over it until Vicki emerges and they squabble over her. This action will be broken up between scenes 4 and 11 in the final script but Cotton writes it here as a single continuous scene.

The action is remarkably similar to that described in the camera script, with almost all dialogue being identical. This is impressive, as various corrections and scribblings on the fly strongly suggest this is Cotton's first draft of episode 2. There are, however, a few differences of note. The first is a practicality: as recorded this scene will not open with the TARDIS being dragged into the square as envisaged here. It will open with us having just missed it being dragged into position, which is far more easily achievable. The typed scene breakdown for episode 2 seems to have already reached this decision.

Cotton's occasional uses of 'hoplite' to indicate a Greek light infantryman are replaced with the rather clearer 'soldier' in the camera script. This is dealt with in Cotton's post-script notes, as is trimming Vicki's entrance line after Cassandra has begged the gods for guidance.

VICKI:

(taking her cue, and having heard last words)

You need my guidance? Speak then...

The cut is probably to avoid the implication she is deliberately attempting to impersonate a god here.

On seeing his recovered trophy, Priam originally chided Paris at slightly greater length.

PRIAM

[...] What are you, a hero or a tourist? Bringing back by-our-lady souvenirs instead of Achilles' body...... Get back to the war.

Later, Paris speaks witheringly of Cassandra's dream in surprisingly modern language:

PARIS

Yes, I hardly think you need trouble an analyst with that one.

Cotton toys with substituting the word 'soothsayer' for 'analyst' here, but the line will later be reworked to avoid either term.

An anachronistic clash of a different kind occurs in a later sequence, where Cotton's Paris possibly hoves a little close to his mythological version:

PRIAM

Your judgement of young women, Paris is notoriously unsound.

PARIS

Not at all. Anyone can tell: she's as innocent as she's pretty.

CASSANDRA

Then give her a golden apple, if you must, and get it over. [...]

The allusion here is to a contest between the goddesses over a golden apple labelled 'to the fairest' which was overseen by Paris and resulted in Paris winning Helen. Depictions of the event entitled 'the Judgement of Paris' became extremely popular in Mediaeval and Renaissance art. It's often surmised this popularity had something to do with the subject matter allowing artists to depict three nude women while retaining a fig leaf of cultured respectability[209].

Perhaps the most significant exchange to **Doctor Who** fans occurs when Priam asks Vicki her name:

VICKI

It's short for Victoria[210].

---

[209] This exchange and another cut speech in which Cassandra calls Paris a 'purblind satyr' and Helen a 'Spartan adulteress' are preserved on pages 63 and 64 of Cotton's novelisation.
[210] This line is later trimmed, thus avoiding fan controversy. In her introductory story Vicki is asked if her name is short for Victoria and replies 'No, just Vicki.'

PRIAM

That's an outlandish sort of name.

CASSANDRA

A heathen name if you ask me....

PRIAM

Nobody did, Cassandra. Well, I really don't think we can call you Victoria, or even Vicki. Far too difficult to remember. We must think of something else. What about... let me see... what about 'Cressida'. Would that suit you?

This offers positive proof of Cressida's presence in the scripts before Vicki's departure was planned. Our first mention of Troilus will follow soon after, in an exchange in which Priam is even harsher to his son than he is on screen.

PRIAM

You get back to the front. If you haven't killed Achilles by nightfall I shall be very seriously displeased.

PARIS

Oh, very well, but I really don't see why Troilus couldn't go? It's more his sort of thing...

PRIAM

Because you are now, heaven help us all, my eldest son and must shoulder – I use the word loosely, of course – your responsibilities. If, by any chance, Achilles should kill **you**, then Troilus will have two elder brothers to avenge; and will fight the better for it. Do you follow?

PARIS

Well, I just wouldn't want to stand in his way, but.....

PRIAM

Now don't argue, Paris; just get out there!

Is it too much of a stretch to consider that this distant father's dismissal of his amorous son might, like *The Tragedy of Phaethon*, reflect something of Cotton's own family?

Paris' line stating he's sought Achilles out but he was 'skulking in his tent', alludes to Achilles' withdrawal from combat before the death of Patroclus in *The Iliad*. Variations on the phrase 'Achilles skulking' (or sulking) 'in his tent' recur regularly in written English through the 19th and 20th centuries[211].

The slightly extended dialogue sequence found in scene 4 is almost entirely reproduced on pages 52 to 54 of Cotton's novelisation. It contains a nice moment for the Doctor where an ethnographic curiosity over the planned method of his execution seems to preclude any sense of fear.

This leads to a speech in which Odysseus says he has been described

---

[211] Sulking is more commonly used but one of many examples of 'skulking' can be found in the following UK Parliamentary exchange from 21 January 1993.

> 'Mr Derek Enright: "Will the Leader of the House undertake the Herculean task of finding the Secretary of State for Education, who these days seems to be skulking like Achilles in his tent?"'

('Business of the House Volume 217').

as an 'uncouth, barbarian pirate'[212] and that he disbelieves 'many stories of myths and monsters' that he has been told on his travels. The chief changes made in the novelisation are the addition of a passage referring to Odysseus' wife Penelope, substituting talk of the Doctor's 'knowledge' for 'almost supernatural power' and the use of the phrase 'two days', rather than the manuscript's 'forty-eight hours'. It's possible this may have seemed out of period, despite the 24-hour clock originating in the ancient world. The camera script has made the same change here.

Scene 5 follows on with Mike and the Doctor now in Odysseus' tent two hours later. Cotton presumably imagined a recording break here. 'Odysseus' is a late substitution for 'Agamemnon's'. A speech in which the Doctor describes the impracticalities of the Wooden Horse as a scheme will be cut from this scene, though the essence is retained in the novelisation[213]. Mention is again made of the 48-hour deadline, with Odysseus stating it's 46 hours now. A brief note later in the notebook alters this to two days and has Odysseus state

---

[212] Odysseus is also described as a pirate in 'Temple of Secrets'. Cotton's conception of Odysseus as a rough pirate probably derives from the account of his sacking numerous cities in *The Iliad* and the commentary on piracy on p486 of *Cambridge Ancient History*, Volume 2, another of Cotton's sources. The distinction between trading and piracy is not clear cut in this period. Polyphemus the Cyclops directly asks Odysseus if he and his men are pirates in *The Odyssey*, and Cotton's decision to highlight the character's piratical nature may have been to foreshadow his interest in acquiring either Vicki or the TARDIS as booty in various versions of the story.
[213] Cotton, *The Myth Makers*, pp69-70.

'Rather less now'[214]. Another post script note inserts Steven (as Mike has now been renamed) reminding the Doctor (and perhaps viewers) that they need to bring about the fall of Troy to rescue Vicki.

Several more lines across this scene are simplified between manuscript and camera script. The most notable trims feature some lurid speculation on how Trojans are currently treating prisoners and Odysseus commending Steven's bravery[215]. One reworked speech rather loses its teeth in the process:

ODYSSEUS

[...] You don't imagine, do you, that, if and when, we enter Troy I shall have time to ask every woman I see if she's a friend of yours, before I slit her throat? It just wouldn't be practical.

The throat-cutting is, perhaps understandably, dropped.

The scene concludes with Odysseus suggesting Mike heads out to get captured wearing his dead friend Diomede's armour. Diomedes is indeed depicted as a friend of Odysseus in *The Iliad* though his death here goes against Homer. In wearing another man's armour Mike echoes Patroclus dressing as Achilles to go into battle[216], though Cotton may also be alluding to another story of Diomedes in which he encounters his old friend Glaucus, now an ally of the

---

[214] This is the form used in the camera script. The novelisation reverts to 48 hours and has Odysseus state it's now reduced to 42. This change in timing will have been to accommodate the rearrangement of some events to allow Homer to move between locations.
[215] Much of this is covered on page 71 of the novelisation.
[216] *The Iliad*, Book XVI, Rieu (pp293-95).

Trojans, on the battlefield and the two men swap armour[217].

Scene 6 finds Paris facing Mike, disguised as Diomede, on the Trojan plain. One exchange, later trimmed, has Paris suggest he and Menelaus could have settled their dispute over Helen like gentlemen. Mike counters that Paris is no gentleman before adding, 'Neither is Menelaus, come to that.' Paris protests at this, pointing out Menelaus is an old friend (rather overlooking his having run away with his wife). The sequence is largely as transmitted, though Paris' description of himself as the 'lion of Troy' does not occur here. Mike comes close to pre-empting it, calling Paris 'a very lion among the Trojans'. While undeniably cowardly, Paris is arguably depicted as a braver man in this scene than in its equivalent in *The Iliad*, where he fires an arrow from distant cover into Diomedes' foot[218].

Scene 7, which joins Priam and Vicki during dinner, establishes the existence of Aeneas and his horsemen, appearing to seed their brief appearance at the end of episode 4. As Aeneas is also pointedly referred to in the handwritten scene breakdown for episode 2, it seems likely his eventual involvement in events was planned from fairly early on. Vicki's surprise that cavalry exists in this period may owe something to Cotton having referred to *Cambridge Ancient History* Volume 2, which indicates the Achaeans had no cavalry[219]. This impression is reinforced by Priam's next speech in which he explains how the Trojans came to Troy, which seems to draw on material about the Dardanians settling in the region from the same

---

[217] *The Iliad* Book VI, p123.
[218] *The Iliad*, Book XI, p207.
[219] Bury, JB, SA Cook and FE Adcock, eds, *Cambridge Ancient History* Volume 2, p484.

volume[220]. A note on the pages following the script pages attempts to slightly simplify and humanise Priam's history of Troy, with input from Vicki. It is simplified again in the camera speech with small sections blanked out including much of this rewrite.

This scene re-establishes Troilus, with it being reported he and Cressida have caught each other's eye off camera. It's been suggested Troilus' non-appearance in episode 2 may have indicated he was a late addition to the story, but this draft now suggests his absence was likely a piece of economic expediency – choosing not to hire an actor for an episode in which they'll play little part[221]. With the exception of the stray additional page referred to earlier, Cotton's notebook drafts end here.

'Small Prophet, Quick Return' – Script and Screen

After a telerecorded recap of the 'Temple of Secrets' cliffhanger played back from film[222], the episode resumes with the Doctor, Steven, Agamemnon and Odysseus at the site of the TARDIS' landing. Several lines, mostly ones given to Ivor Salter as Odysseus, survive in the camera script for this scene but do not feature in the finished episode. The omissions are handled fairly smoothly, which to me

---

[220] Bury, Cook, Adcock, *Cambridge Ancient History* Volume 2, pp487-90.

[221] Odysseus is the only guest character to appear throughout the story. Achilles appears in only episodes 1 and 4, Menelaus in only episodes 1 and 3, Agamemnon is absent from episode 4 and Priam, Paris and Cassandra are all absent from episode 1.

[222] The recap ends before the pre-credits camera zoom-in on the Trojan plaque.

suggests the lines may have been dropped during the technical run rather than during recording[223].

The first skipped section has Odysseus suggest Agamemnon's interactions with the Doctor and Steven will become the basis of songs sung around the fire, making explicit the notion of real events being fictionalised by bards that underpins much of *The Myth Makers* and a good deal of Homeric scholarship[224]. Also hopped over later is a brief exchange during which Odysseus' scepticism and Achilles religiosity are highlighted[225]. While we may slightly regret losing these moments, dropping them does speed the scene up[226].

In another missing sequence, already absent from the camera script,

---

[223] Though Salter can be heard starting to speak at one point as Francis de Wolff runs two speeches together.

[224] Cotton retains the line in his novelisation (Cotton, *The Myth Makers* p49).

[225] One of the six lines in this script to refer to gods or goddesses is found in this untransmitted dialogue. In this instance 'Gods' is spelled with an uppercase G, in a shortened version of Odysseus' line about Achilles seeing gods everywhere.

[226] Andrew Pixley has suggested the lines were skipped in error by the actors during recording, with the later exchange being trimmed as a result of two of Odysseus' speeches ending with a similar cue '...who are you?' (Pixley, Andrew, 'Silent Witnesses', *Nothing at the End of the Lane* #1, p95). This is also possible, but it's perhaps surprising that no attempt was made to quickly remount the sequence, given this is the first scene of the episode. My hunch is that Ivor Salter may have been struggling with some of the material here, and Michael Leeston-Smith recognised this and chose to work 'round these difficult dialogue sections. Leeston-Smith would have been familiar with Salter and his work, having previously cast him as a belligerent drunk in *Affray,* a 1962 episode of **Z Cars**.

Agamemnon originally granted a request from Odysseus to question the now confirmed spies before he leaves, an exchange which makes his departure seem slightly less hurried.

Evidence this scene has been extensively reworked can be found in the script's instruction '(**ONTO PAGE 5**)' at the foot of page 3. There's a further trim on page 5 of the camera script, where the Doctor's whispered words about Vicki to Steven were originally longer.

The next scene (labelled in the script as scene 4/5[227]) is broadly the opening of scene 3 from the notebook manuscript in which the TARDIS has been brought to the Trojan square.

Scene 6 features Vicki (now treated as anxious from the start of the scene) watching the TARDIS 'scanners' and being alarmed as Priam's face comes into view '(RATHER LIKE "BIG BROTHER IS WATCHING YOU")'[228]. The suggestion Vicki could hear what's been said outside seems to have been lost now[229].

---

[227] Again, I'm unsure why the scene numbering jumps. It's possible it was originally planned to open this sequence with scenes establishing the TARDIS in transit and Vicki reacting within.

[228] Stage direction from p9 of the 'Small Prophet, Quick Return' camera script. We have no manuscript treatment of these Vicki insert scenes which break up the action in the Trojan square, so this may be Donald Tosh's work.

[229] The 2001 audio narration on *The Myth Makers* soundtrack release suggests Vicki leaves the TARDIS in scene 11 after being alarmed by discussion outside, but the script has her alarmed by Priam looming up on the screen and looking at Steven's old clothes before any talk of the talk of burning the TARDIS takes place. We next find her already in the TARDIS living quarters pulling items from the wardrobe with no indication she's heard, or can currently hear, any

Scene 7 sees Cassandra tell of a prophetic dream in which some kind of gift from the Greeks is brought into Troy but turns out to contain enemy soldiers, though she interprets the TARDIS as this gift. This moment derails any intent there may have been to offer a purely rationalist version of the Troy story, devoid of gods or magic. Cassandra's prophecy is correct (and ignored) as tradition demands, but the nature of her gift and the way it's routinely dismissed go completely unexamined.

A small edit appears to have been made to the end of the scene after recording, presumably to bring the episode down to the correct length. After Cassandra recommends the TARDIS be burned, Paris protests that it's his property, but is overruled by Priam who agrees with Cassandra. There's an outside possibility the scene ending was removed because it features a rare instance of Cassandra being listened to, but this seems unlikely[230].

Scene 8 depicts the TARDIS wardrobe. From the script's description it appears, as it had in *The Space Museum*, as a small cupboard.

Scene 9 again finds Ivor Salter appearing to struggle with his lines, paraphrasing his final speech and rather losing the sense of another

---

of the conversation outside. The implication is it's Priam examining the ship that's led Vicki to follow Steven's example and exit in period appropriate dress. The cutting of Vicki's draft script entrance line in scene 11 reinforces her not having followed the Trojans' arguments.

[230] 'Small Prophet, Quick Return' camera script, p13. An edit of this kind was a very rare occurrence, requiring precision to keep the material in phase and having major cost implications. A splice to the tape made it subsequently unusable in an era when videotape was extremely expensive and so routinely wiped and reused.

by swapping the words 'effrontery' and 'credulity'. Salter losing his way here may reflect late changes or have some bearing on the trims made to his first scene.

It's probably worth stressing that William Hartnell generally sticks very closely to his script throughout *The Myth Makers*, with none of the vague paraphrasing of lines we see at the end of *Galaxy 4*. Hartnell having just returned refreshed from a summer break, having a fairly small role in the story, or being keen to impress a fairly illustrious guest cast may be factors here.

At the scene's end, stage directions indicate there's no scene 10, presumably due to a cut earlier in production. As there are only two clear story strands at this point, this was probably an establishing shot of Troy.

Scene 11 features the conclusion of the long Trojan square scene discussed further in manuscript form. One notable addition is a stage direction relating to Cyclops placed in the section to the left of the script that principally covers cues, cameras moves and changing artist positions.

Cyclops is not mentioned in the more discursive and writerly stage directions which intersperse the dialogue to the right, suggesting this note flagging Cyclops' presence may have been established by the director. Page 22, on which this scene ends and the next begins, concludes after the new scene header and opening stage directions with the words '**(ONTO PAGE 24)**'[231]. This points to earlier parts of this next scene having been heavily revised and considerably shortened[232].

The first stage direction for scene 12 is repeated at the top on page 24. Here Steven suggests the Wooden Horse as a means to end the war and the Doctor rejects the idea.

As previously established, there are a number of trims made to this scene, some of which can be identified through blanked out passages. However, the pages most changed from the manuscript version are pages 25 and 26. Page 25 also features a series of mangled spellings of Odysseus in speech headers, suggesting hurriedly typed revisions that have been faithfully transcribed.

The reworked material here inserts a messenger announcing that Paris is seeking a duel with Achilles (currently a skulking non-combatant) or a willing substitute. New dialogue establishes that Paris is a puny coward who hates killing. This now informs Steven's plan to get captured, perhaps making his scheme seem less hare-brained.

The camera script indicates no recording break between this scene and scene 13, also in studio, in which Paris faces Steven on the plain,

---

[231] Although there are no obvious changes to page 22, it too appears to have been retyped. 'Gods' is capitalised in Cassandra's final speech, which also uses the word 'lightening' where 'lightning' is intended and the word 'usury' in the place of 'usurp'. It's possible this page was amended when the direction regarding Cyclops was inserted, which runs alongside Cassandra's slightly misspelled lines.
[232] If the last page of scene 12 had needed enough revision to be retyped, the instruction to skip a page would have come there.

now in Greek armour.[233] If taken literally, this suggests Peter Purves was dressed in this new costume in the space of around 50 seconds.

As he remains seated for much of scene 12, and doesn't appear to be framed in long shot when standing, it's possible with careful camera work that he could have already been wearing some elements of the armour that might go undetected. However, unless he was wearing a cloak, I suspect it's far more likely that a short undocumented break occurred at this point.[234].

The title Paris gives himself, 'lion of Troy', sounds suitably Classical and time-honoured, and although lions are repeatedly referred to poetically in The Iliad (and a lion hunt is famously depicted on a knife at Mycenae), I've not been able to locate a use of the phrase in earlier texts. Homer tends to use similes comparing the acts of heroes to the behaviour of lions and Paris is never considered worthy of this treatment.

Scene 14 features a small trim to the middle of Priam's lines

---

[233] Sadly, Purves' recollection of scene 13's fight with Barrie Ingham as Paris taking place on location at Frensham Little Pond (Here's One I Wrote Earlier, p97) doesn't tally with either the camera script or the rough shooting schedule assembled from available data (Bignell, Richard, Doctor Who on Location, pp15-16 and note on p25). Purves and Ingham did both shoot at this location, but the detailed camera script and sound quality of this sequence indicate it was recorded in the studio. Purves' memory of the fight being a night shoot (direct message chat with the author, 20 April 2023) suggests he's thinking of the sequence where Steven approaches the Greek camp in episode 1.

[234] Peter Purves has no recollection of a quick costume change (direct message chat, 20 April 2023).

exhorting Vicki to relate the legend she's reminded of on p33. Two lines have been blanked out, leaving the word 'future' hanging at the start of the next line. In the notebook manuscript this incompletely trimmed clause is, 'If you're telling me the truth, and you really do come from the future.' Bar the trims to Priam's explanation of how the Trojans came to Troy and Mike's name changing to Steven, this scene is essentially unchanged from the earlier draft.

Episode 3 – Written Breakdown

Donald Cotton's handwritten scene breakdown for episode 3 does not get very far. Scene 1 was to open on a set representing part of Agamemnon's ship. Vicki and the Trojan women are being taken on board (presumably Andromache, Cassandra and Hecuba). Mike (replacing a crossed out 'DR. Who') manages to tell Vicki to trust the Doctor as he says farewell, and after thanking the Greek heroes for their efforts, Agamemnon sets sail with his booty.

Scene 2 has the Doctor, Odysseus, Menelaus and Helen on the beach. After the reunited couple leave, the Doctor tries persuading Odysseus to sail after Agamemnon and rescue Vicki, but Odysseus just wants to get home to Ithaca. The scene breakdown breaks down here, with the unfulfilled possibility of allusions to *The Trojan Women* and *The Odyssey* ahead. There will be no handwritten scene breakdown for episode 4.

Episode 3 – Typed Breakdown

The typed scene breakdown for episode 3 continues smoothly from where the script of 'Small Prophet, Quick Return' leaves off. In scene 1, Vicki prophesies Troy will be destroyed if Mike is killed, and Priam accordingly prevents their execution. Vicki and Mike are instead placed under house address for 24 hours with a promise their lives will be spared if Troy prevails.

Scene 2 finds the Doctor trying to devise a means to take Troy. He dismisses siege engines as anachronistic, just as Donald Cotton had in his background notes for the serial. Here he and the Doctor take their lead from HL Lorimer's *Homer and the Monuments*, which describes the Wooden Horse as 'a fiction based on a perverted notion of a siege-engine', believing it to be drawn from the era of *The Odyssey's* composition rather than the actual period of the Trojan War[235]. Odysseus' spy reports Mike's capture in Troy, and, realising he needs to act quickly, the Doctor suggests the Wooden Horse. Odysseus agrees to the plan on the condition he gets the credit if it succeeds, and insists the Doctor accompanies him in the Horse. Odysseus' demanding credit rather deftly takes care of the scheme being credited to him in legend.

Scene 3 has Odysseus' spy in Trojan disguise telling Mike and Vicki that the Doctor intends to rescue them in the next 24 hours. They tell the spy to delay the attack, explaining that if Troy does fall in that time they'll be executed. Unfortunately, scene 4 sees the spy killed trying to leave Troy.

Scene 5 has the Horse being set up on the beach before being positioned outside Troy. Instructing the Doctor to join him and his men in the Horse, Odysseus orders the Greek fleet to sail away and return at night. Scene 6 in Priam's palace has the Trojans discover the Greeks have gone and left them the Horse.

The sketchy nature of how the scenario is visualised at this stage,

---

[235] Lorimer, HL, *Homer and the Monuments*, p522.

and how speedily this document appears to have been typed, is well conveyed by the line 'everyone dashes to the window (or whatever) and see [sic] the deserted beach'. Even as they write this sentence, the breakdown's author seems to be acknowledging a besieged palace surrounded by high city walls is likely to be short of windows overlooking the coast. The conversational nature of this leads me to suspect the document is recording an unfolding discussion. A model shot of the Horse is proposed here. Cassandra predicts disaster 'but as always is told to shut up'. Neatly, Cassandra having been wrong about the TARDIS bringing doom is used to justify ignoring her. Vicki and Mike are released, with Mike warning Vicki they're still in danger because the Trojan Horse will bring about the city's destruction.

Scene 7 sees the huge Horse's legs being pulled by rope up to the city, with faint sounds of armour and the 'Doctor's 'Hmms' etc.' audible within[236].

Once again, the broad shape of the televised episode is discernible in this breakdown, which clearly contradicts most elements of Cotton's anecdote about Cyclops, revealing his plot function to have been clearly established prior to the scripting of episode 3. The speed with which the Wooden Horse is constructed still seems remarkable, an issue the script for episode 3 will attempt to address in dialogue.

---

[236] Lucas Testro suggests this familiarity with Hartnell's performance tics is evidence pointing towards Donald Tosh having authored or co-written this document, noting that Cotton's wife Hilary doesn't recall him watching a great deal of TV, not even seeing his own **Doctor Who** episodes transmitted.

'Death of a Spy' – Script and Screen

'Death of a Spy', the title eventually given episode 3, is surely an attempt at audience misdirection, first appearing on screen under the caption 'NEXT EPISODE' at the end of 'Small Prophet, Quick Return' just as Steven and Vicki seem likely to be killed for spying. The subterfuge probably didn't deceive much of the audience, which would have been several weeks away from imagining **Doctor Who** companions could die mid-adventure. Donald Cotton recalls the original title given this episode being 'Is There a Doctor in the Horse?' In Cotton's colourful telling of that title being vetoed, he described it as 'being greeted with bared gums'[237]. Donald Tosh's recollection is slightly different, recalling episode 4 as having been proposed as 'A Doctor in the Horse', but that 'Johnny Wiles wouldn't have it because he didn't like these little jokes.'[238] The joke here is a play on the cry 'Is there a doctor in the house?' legendarily supposed to go out where someone becomes seriously ill in the theatre.

Scene 1 continues directly from the end of 'Small Prophet, Quick Return', the end of which is played back from a telerecording. Priam's reference to 'Hercules' here is strictly speaking anachronistic as this is the Latin form of the name of the Greek demigod, Heracles. This seems to be a choice made in the interests of clarity. Cotton can happily write of Heracles in *The Golden Fleece* for the Third Programme, but a mass audience would have known the name Hercules better. Paris' suggestion that his father look up Diomede in 'the Greek Army List' to see how impressive a catch he is, may be a jokey reference to Homer's exhaustive list of the principal Greek

---

[237] Walker, *Talkback: The Sixties*, p171.
[238] Evans, 'Script Editing **Who**: Donald Tosh', p11.

122

combatants, 'The Catalogue of Ships'[239]. The scene also contains the first explicit acknowledgement in the scripts of Cassandra's legendary reputation as a prophetess whose predictions always go unheeded as Paris calls her 'a fortune teller of notorious unreliability'.

In Scene 2, the very start of Odysseus' line about catapults and a sentence from the middle of the Doctor's explanation of how catapults work have been blanked out. The sense of the latter may be preserved in his slightly lengthier and looser explanation in the novel[240].

The script for scene 3 sees a use of 'your' for 'you're' in dialogue on page 10, which seems to me out of place for Cotton and suggests editorial input: 'you're' is correctly used later in the scene on page 14.

Scene 4 finally offers a sop to those of us worried about how quickly

---

[239] *The Iliad*, Book II (pp52-59 in the Rieu translation).

[240] Cotton, *The Myth Makers*, p91. If the novelisation does accurately reflect an earlier script version, this suggests Cotton may have retained a draft of episode 3 of *The Myth Makers* in addition to the scripts listed by Bonhams. There's circumstantial evidence from Cotton's 1984 DWASocial 5 interview that might support this. Cotton speaks of rewriting the second half of *The Gunfighters* novelisation without access to the last two scripts, which were lost. It's likely he means his personal copies here (the BBC's copies survive), suggesting he may have novelised his two serials without access to BBC held scripts. He certainly seems to stop working from onscreen dialogue in his reinvention of *The Gunfighters*' later action. If so, his closer adherence to elements of screen dialogue throughout *The Myth Makers* novelisation might suggest he had personal copies of the scripts for all four episodes to hand.

the Wooden Horse is built as Odysseus explains he has 'half a company' of craftsmen on standby to construct whatever machine the Doctor devises.

Scene 5 establishes that both Vicki and Troilus are under 17 years old. It's even possible Vicki may be younger than 16.

TROILUS

I'm seventeen ... next birthday!

VICKI

But that's hardly any better than me. You shouldn't be killing at that age.

These ages may seem implausible given both of the performers are clearly in their 20s, but this is what the text expects us to believe and hopes 40-line television images will persuade us of. The novelisation, possibly in the interests of propriety, has them both approaching 18.

Scenes 6 and 9 both lapse into calling the Doctor '**DOCTOR:** ' rather than '**DOCTOR WHO**: ' but it's hard to identify any major rewrites to scene 6 by examining Donald Cotton's novelisation[241]. Scene 9 features a couple of small trims in the middle of the Doctor's lines worrying about the Horse's fetlocks and the danger of it collapsing. If we can rely on Cotton's novelisation, these excised passages featured him worrying further about whether the construction is mechanically sound[242].

Odysseus' punning wordplay linking the Horse and 'a mare's nest' is

---

[241] Scene 6 also sees this episode's sole mentions of gods. It's capitalised, again suggesting rewrites.
[242] Cotton, *The Myth Makers*, p123.

anachronistic and obviously wouldn't work in Greek. However, there is a more egregious example of English language punning still to come before the episode ends.

In scene 8, Odysseus' reference to 'a Bacchante at her first orgy' is anachronistic. Bachantes were what the Romans called the frenzied female followers of the god Bacchus. However, the Greek version of these women were known as Maenads and followed Dionysus, the Greek god of wine.

It should also be stated that while the word 'orgy' has come to be primarily associated with sexual activity in modern English, it covered a multitude of sins in the Classical world. For the Greeks the word related to exactly the kind of wild Dionysiac worship that Maenads performed. The joke is, in consequence, exactly as rude as you'd like it to be.

Scene 14 is another in which Odysseus' dialogue is slightly paraphrased, in this case obscuring the sense of its final line. On-screen Odysseus says 'Well, this time Troy will be destroyed,' rather than the scripted 'This time tomorrow – Troy will destroyed,' which would have reminded viewers of the deadline facing Vicki and Steven.

In scene 15, despite my suspicions that the palace of Priam would not have a window through which the Greek lines could be overlooked, the script's stage directions have the Trojans going to just such a window[243].

Thankfully, the camera directions on the script's left side make clear this is up a series of steps, a feature of the set remembered by designer John Wood[244].

Scene 18 features the often quoted exchange 'Then woe to the House of Priam! Woe to the Trojans.' 'It's too late to say whoa to the horse...' It's a piece of English language wordplay that makes a mockery of this otherwise highly sensible serial. Oddly, the camera script elects to spell 'whoa' as 'woe' here, with the typist possibly missing the joke.

Episode 4 – Typed Breakdown

The breakdown opens with an establishing model shot of the TARDIS, Wooden Horse and guards in the Trojan square, before moving to scene 1 in which Priam, Mike and 'Viki' observe it from a

---

[243] Part of palace interior is visible behind the doors of the palace portico on a surviving set photo. The fact the palace portico stands in front of the Trojan square suggests the featured palace interior would have been depicted on screen as being more at less on ground level. Once the palace being surrounded by the mighty walls of Troy is factored in, sight lines start to become an issue.
[244] 'John Wood Interview', *The Frame* #23/24, p67. The palace staircase appears to be the short set of stairs that can be seen in two set images. When viewed full on, we can see these steps lead up to a forced perspective painted flat which depicts further stairs heading to a half open door. In the studio, actors would only have been able to ascend four or five feet before coming up against this flat, so scenes featuring the characters heading to and from what he later discovers is the palace balcony would have required careful shooting.

palace window and Priam pardons the travellers. Mike and Vicki resolve to make contact with the occupants of the Horse to get news of the Doctor.

Scene 2 is set inside the Horse. Odysseus refuses to let the Doctor go and look for Mike and Vicki until their scheme has successfully concluded, further rationalising his decision by pointing out the Doctor will be unable to leave the Horse unseen.

Scene 3 has 'Vicky and Michael' by a leg of the Horse, trying to contact those within without alerting the guards by 'calling gently and tapping'. The change from Mike to Michael here is curious. Vicki's name is also misspelled, but that's not uncommon across this document.

In scene 4, prevented from answering by a suspicious Odysseus, the Doctor resorts to communicating with his friends through 'gentle morse-code'. Scene 5 sees 'Mike and Vicky' finally recognise the Doctor's 'morse-code' and reply rustily, because by their time Morse code 'is just a childs [sic] game'. Overall, this sequence seems both rather contrived and potentially very slow when dramatised. It's not entirely surprising the Morse idea is dropped before the final script.

Scene 6 has Priam in his palace asking for Mike and Vicki. He becomes suspicious on learning they are by the Horse. He orders them be brought to him, before telling Helen that, now the war is over, he's going to make arrangements to have her given back to Menelaus. This scene also features the dismissal and return of Cassandra again, giving the impression it may have been thought up as it was being typed up. Her return may signify that the latter portion of the scene has been deliberated devised to feature Helen and Cassandra together, for reasons the breakdown fails to

127

elaborate on. It's conceivable Cassandra would have prophesied Helen's actual fate here (possibly as depicted by Aeschylus), but I've no textual evidence to support this supposition.

In Scene 7 night is falling and 'Michael and Vicky' have just finished 'there' Morse chat with the Doctor and arranged to meet him once the fighting starts '(at the Tardis?)'. The use of 'there' for 'their' reinforces my suspicion this document was not directly authored by Cotton, whose handwritten spelling and grammar are solid (though he does spell siege 'seige'). This typo strikes me as the kind of slip it's very easy to make when taking another's dictation and not being clear what the next word may be. The travellers are instructed to attend King Priam, but, realising this may make escaping harder during the fighting, they choose to hide at the edge of the square. The breakdown specifies this sequence is to be followed by stock footage of the Greek ships returning and the Greeks quietly disembarking.

In scene 8 'Vicky and Michael' watch Greeks descend from the Horse and overpower its guards. Scene 9 has Priam wondering why Mike and Vicki still haven't come to him. Cassandra tells him 'I told you so – 'Watch that horse!''. The fact this dialogue is quoted rather than reported may suggest it was seen as a key moment.

Scene 10 sees the Doctor appearing in the square as the last man to leave the horse. He heads to 'Tardis'. There is then 'General Mellee as Gate has been opened'. 'Mike and Vicky' try to cross the square but Vicki is captured by a 'greek(who doesn't realise she isn't a Trojan wench' [sic]. I suspect the voice, if not the hand, of Cotton is involved the hurriedly typed phrase 'Trojan wench' which recalls the 'serving wenches' in the handwritten draft and camera script of episode 1. Mike then rescues 'Vicky' but she then remembers she's left a keepsake from Helen in the palace and rushes off for that. Mike continues to the TARDIS. In unscripted form, Vicki's actions here feel distinctly flimsily motivated.

Scene 11 finds Vicki in the palace, forced to hide when Priam and Achilles enter, fighting. Achilles is limping badly (presumably from an ankle injury) and collapses from loss of blood. Priam is about to finish Achilles off when Odysseus enters and kills him. Odysseus then discovers Vicki and takes her captive. This feels potentially too strong for 1960s **Doctor Who**, though Priam is, once again, fortunate to avoid being beaten to death with his dead grandson.

In Scene 12 the Doctor and Mike witness the fighting from the TARDIS. They spot Odysseus with Vicki and head out to rescue her.

Scene 13 sees the fighting more or less over- 'just general looting going on prior to the burning of the city'. Odysseus reluctantly gives up Vicki. Agamemnon arrives and congratulates the Doctor on the success of their mission and 'Menalaeos' is reunited with Helen. The scene breakdown says 'rather unwillingly' but doesn't make clear whether this applies to one or both of them. The 'Doctor, Mike and Viky' leave in the TARDIS, impressing 'Odd' with the ship's dematerialisation and leading him to believe they were 'Gods' after all.

The finale proposed by this scene breakdown seems to present a number of problems. The Morse Code element feels undramatic and farfetched. Characters seem arbitrarily moved around and the Doctor takes little part in the action, only remaining to the story's end because Vicki is left behind. On top of this, the story appears to peter out anticlimactically after the slaughter of the Trojan royals, and, based on the summary presented here, runs the risk of presenting the regular characters as rather callous – orchestrating, and standing by to witness, a massacre.

'Horse of Destruction' – Script and Screen

This final episode is the one which Donald Tosh recalled initially being entitled 'A Doctor in the Horse'. Lacking the questioning framing Cotton remembered, this version of the title fits the plot of episode 4 better. However, it is diminished as a play on words, by not evoking 'Is there a doctor in the house?'[245]

In this episode alone, the telerecorded cliffhanger from the previous episode is given its own scene number in the script, marked as 'Scene I', before the episode proper begins in scene 2. Scene 2 resumes in Priam's palace with action again appearing continuous. For the first time, stage directions to the right, rather than left, of the script mention there being a staircase here. The top of these stairs now appears to lead to a balcony from which the Horse can be better viewed.

This new information about the setting may appear because the writer had not greatly considered the layout of the palace set prior to this episode, but it's also possible this awareness of the set's layout derives from the scene having been rewritten after it was designed by someone familiar with the set.

We can be confident this scene has undergone some rewriting thanks to it introducing the Doctor's new companion Katarina, a

---

[245] Or even the popular movie from a decade previously, *Doctor in the House* (1954).

previously unseen and unmentioned handmaid of Cassandra[246], whose character would not have been devised when Cotton delivered his script for this episode on 28 July. Katarina's name alone indicates she's a late addition to the scheme of things – it appears nowhere in the literature of Troy, and bucks the trend of Achilles, Cassandra, Cressida, Cyclops, Hector and even Hecuba in the various iterations of *The Myth Makers,* by using a K for its hard C sound. The Homeric period appears to considerably predate use of the name Katarina or other similar variants on Catherine, so, if the production team had been striving at this late stage for strict accuracy, she'd have more likely been called Aikaterini.[247]

A brief scene, 2A, follows showing Vicki freeing Steven from the dungeon. The numbering, which indicates it's a late addition, allows scene numbers to be retained for the rest of the script.

Scene 3 has Odysseus and the Doctor in discussion within the Horse. While there's little of significance in the dialogue, there is one notable format change which is maintained for most of the episode that follows. In previous episodes the Doctor's dialogue has been almost exclusively preceded by '**DOCTOR WHO**:' in the script, but here he's simply '**DOCTOR**:', strongly suggesting a change of

---

[246] Cassandra speaks of the Gods with a capital G on the previous page, which, as I've hopefully now established, strongly suggests a revision.

[247] A name believed to derive, like Catherine, from the Greek root relating to purity or purification that also gives us the word catharsis.

authorship[248].

There are no scenes 4 or 5. I presume they were either an earlier treatment of Vicki freeing Steven or originally dealt with the transportation of the Horse.

In later years, Donald Tosh recalled cutting a section of script that would most likely occurred here or at the opening of scene 6:

> 'I remember, in the script – there was one scene were [sic] the horse is being pulled into Troy, and Cassandra appears on the palace balcony, and when she sees this horse she starts saying "It's an omen. An omen of disaster," and then she says "Prove that I am right. Give me a sign," and, suddenly, out of nowhere, a vast pile of steaming horse shit appeared. She looks and she says "Oh, yes, oh yes! The auguries are bad." And I thought "this has got to go!"'[249]

While I can well believe Donald Cotton gave some thought to toilet arrangements within the Wooden Horse, I'd be surprised if he ever seriously considered a scene like this suitable for teatime television. There may be a germ of truth to the story, but without further

---

[248] This is by no means conclusive, but is strongly suggestive. Donald Tosh's script for episode 1 of *The Massacre* (1966) features '**DOCTOR WHO:**', '**DOCTOR:**', '**DR.:**' and '**DOCTOR: WHO:**' (where I presume he wrote '**DOCTOR:**' before remembering he was supposed to write '**DOCTOR WHO:**'), and while episode 4 predominantly uses '**DOCTOR:**', '**DOCTOR WHO:**' does occasionally appear. The evidence is muddied by the complex authorship of *The Massacre* and we always have to consider the vagaries of the intermediary secretaries who will have prepared these scripts for duplication.
[249] Stevens, 'Donald Tosh Interview'.

evidence I feel inclined to treat Tosh's 'vast pile of steaming horse shit' as mythical.

Katarina next appears on page 9 of the script, in scene 7 which takes place in the Trojan square. She's only mentioned by name in the left-hand camera directions but Vicki and Steven continue to discuss her over the next two pages, establishing Katarina is a character known to Vicki (although, as with Troilus we have missed their first meeting). These pages are numbered 9a and 9b, indicating they're a late addition to the script, almost certainly made by Tosh[250]. This scene also reinforces Steven's awareness of Vicki's affection for Troilus and will motivate her ruse to ensure he is out of Troy when the Greeks attack.

Scene 8 actually begins towards the end of page 9b, following a short model shot of the Horse and the TARDIS played in from film. This seems to indicate additional work has also been done to this scene, though seemingly not enough to further throw out the page

---

[250] Further evidence pointing toward Donald Tosh reworking this sequence (and indeed much of episode 4) includes Steven capitalising the word 'Gods' on page 9. This scene does not appear in Donald Cotton's novelisation, which by this point is increasingly tackling sequences without reported speech, and reworking material to better incorporate the character of Homer. The fact the novelisation tells its version of 'Horse of Destruction' briskly with no apparent reference to its onscreen dialogue (Cotton, *The Myth Makers* pp126-40) may also indicate Tosh rewrote it extensively, meaning the script the Bonhams catalogue suggests Cotton held for episode 4 may not have been much use to him. It's equally possible the brisk summary of the events of episode 4 arises from Cotton approaching his agreed word count and wanting to rattle speedily towards the story's conclusion.

numbers. Unfortunately, the additional two pages in scene 7 seem to have an adverse knock-on effect. The episode now appears to run slightly too long for its time slot, and approximately two pages of material need to be lost after recording. As scene 7 establishes Vicki getting Steven to hide behind some pillars in the square and introduces the idea of Vicki saving Troilus, it needs to be retained in full.

This leaves scene 8 as the only portion of the recording that features material that can be cut without damaging the flow of the plot. The production team appears to have applied the writing maxim 'start late, finish early' in its edits, removing the opening and closing sections of this scene within Priam's palace[251]. This means we lose an opening in which Katarina has returned to tell Cassandra that she's been unable to find Vicki anywhere. This cut may have made Katarina's presence in the last scene, and unexplained reappearance here, seem slightly jarring on transmission.

The cut sequence continues with Priam descend from observing the Horse on his balcony, slightly underwhelmed by its aesthetics. Paris feels this is inappropriate:

PARIS

But father, we mustn't look a gift from the God's in the

---

[251] The narration on the BBC audio release of *The Myth Makers* relocates this scene to the square, presumably to reflect the crowd sounds under the action. This was intended to have been sound coming through from the balcony and gradually reducing in volume as the scene progressed, but this is less clear after the scene's opening is cut. This scene's indoor location is, however, clarified by Cassandra's line stating the Horse is 'out there'.

mouth.[252]

It's a great gag, which it's a shame to lose.

After Priam has begun to express misgivings about the Horse's divine nature, which Cassandra backs, the scene as transmitted opens with Troilus entering to reveal Steven has escaped his cell. Vicki re-enters soon after, denying any involvement in Steven's escape. She is left in the care of Katarina as the Trojan royals go to the square, distressed by the thought of the Trojans she's come to care for being massacred. This is where the transmitted scene ends. However, in the script it continues:

(KATARINA CROSSING TO THE BALCONY AND LOOKING OUT)

KATARINA

Have you seen the horse? The high priestess Cassandra, believes it will bring about Troy's downfall.

VICKI (PULLING HERSELF TOGETHER)

I'm sure it won't. How did you become one of Cassandra's handmaids?

KATARINA

Through the auguries. It was foretold that I should be, and it has been fortold [sic] that I shall not.

---

[252] 'Horse of Destruction' camera script, p10. The capitalisation and erroneously placed apostrophe lead me to suspect Donald Tosh's hand in this sequence. Though the joke itself feels very much like Cotton (and one begging to be made), it's reproduced nowhere in his novelisation.

135

VICKI

What do you mean?

KATARINA (MATTER OF FACTLY)

I am going to die.

VICKI

To die! But how can you tell – are you ill.

KATARINA

No. But I shall die. The signs have been given.

VICKI

Signs?

KATARINA

My own pet dove flew backwards to his nest, then beat his wings thrice and dies. When we examined him he had no liver. So I shall die-

(FADE TO BLACK)[253]

The loss of this scene is significant. Soon after Katarina had been devised as a replacement for Vicki it was realised her origins at the edge of prehistory presented a problem for science fiction narratives. It had presumably been imagined that Katarina's faith in mythic gods might offer a filter through which she could comprehend futuristic marvels, but in the event this proved

---

[253] 'Horse of Destruction', pp13-14. I've reproduced the script as presented, preserving minor typos.

impractical. As Donald Tosh explained:

> '...with regard to Katarina, I realised the character we had created wasn't going to work when I started reading Paul Erickson's early scripts for *The Ark* [1966], and it was very clear what the problem was. Everything had to be explained to this girl. And I mean, absolutely everything, because she came from a primitive and distant past and was being transported to a far distant future. And I said, "We can't do this! Every story will be dragged down again and again to make room for explanations." Everything needed explaining.'[254]

By the time Adrienne Hill came to be cast as Katarina her fate was already sealed. She was to be quickly killed off (in part because *The Daleks' Master Plan* offered no safe haven in which she might be left) and be replaced by a new character, Sara, who'd be more capable of grasping future technology. Thus, the first material Hill shot as Katarina was her death scene[255]. The decision to make Katarina a stopgap, did however offer the production team this opportunity to dramatically foreshadow her death. It's unfortunate then that this scene is cut, as the edit makes Katarina's later statements in which she seems to presume she's now died seem to spring from

---

[254] Stevens, 'Donald Tosh Interview'.
[255] Filmed at Ealing on the 27 September 1965, three days before the recording of 'Small Profit, Quick Return'. It's perhaps fitting, given the way Cressida derives from stories of trading of women like property, that **Doctor Who** should swap Vicki for Katarina and then Sara as cursorily as Agamemnon swapped Chryseis for Briseis.

nowhere[256].

Scene 9 is notable chiefly for finally making explicit on screen that Odysseus' motivation for being part of the Trojan campaign is the self-centred pursuit of booty, previous allusions to which have been cut. The revelation allows the Doctor to take a clear moral position at last and protest against the mass killing he has largely contrived.

Scene 10, in which Vicki sends Troilus out of the city in order to spare the Trojan's life, seems to have had a cursory rewrite to insert Katarina while preserving its original form. She is seen sleeping at the scene's opening as Troilus enters. My suspicion is the rest of this scene is largely as Donald Cotton originally scripted it. When Vicki asks Troilus to capture Diomede, he asks if she's in love with the Greek, the story's strongest suggestion yet of the traditional love triangle between Diomede, Cressida and Troilus.

Scene 11 features the Greeks leaving the Horse and slaying its guards, their descent via rope being covered by a film insert. The Doctor's uneasy position in the narrative is reinforced in one of scene 11's stage directions – 'THE DOCTOR IS CLEARLY NOT HAPPY WITH THE KILLING'.

The next sequence is a telecine insert of material filmed on location that has not been given a scene number. This means the fight scene it involves can be shot with greater dynamism, and that Cavan Kendall will not be required in studio as Achilles after his work on 'Temple of Lies'.

Troilus discovers Achilles hiding on the plain and, thinking Vicki may

---

[256] There is no trace of Katarina's foretold end in Cotton's novelisation. It's quite possible he was unaware of it.

have led him into a trap, asks 'Has Cressida played me faulse?' On this occasion I wonder if the apparent spelling error might be deliberate. The notion of playing false is one that recurs in Shakespeare, and the spelling of false here echoes that found in some of his work[257]. As Shakespeare's Cressida is famed for falsehood, it may be a deliberate nod to the playwright is intended here[258]. Whether the Shakespearean allusion is intended not, it seems this line is meant to offer us the 'true' reason for Cressida gaining her reputation. Achilles' last line also seems to recall Shakespeare, with his 'The wheel has spun full circle' evoking 'the wheel is come full circle' from *King Lear*[259]. Troilus' response – 'I live to call down wrath for love of Cressida!' may conceivably be playing the phrase 'the wrath of love' in *As You Like It*[260]. The proliferation of Shakespearean allusions in Cotton's novels for Target lead me to suspect this is his largely unedited work.

The fight ends with Achilles catching his foot in undergrowth, losing balance and being killed by Troilus. His ankle has, as anticipated in earlier scene breakdowns, proven his undoing, though his killer and the exact manner of his dispatch are somewhat unexpected. Troilus is badly wounded by the dying Greek, his injury perhaps offering a reason for Vicki to stay and care for him, in a mirror of the wounding

---

[257] See Sonnets 68 and 127.

[258] This may seem unlikely but U seems unlikely to be typed in error when writing the word 'false', being some distance from both A or L on the typewriter keyboard, and James Lynn's theatrical pronunciation of the word does seem to strongly sound the U.

[259] Act V, scene 3.

[260] Act V, scene 2.

of Diomedes in Benoît de Sainte-Maure[261].

Scene 12 sees the gates of Troy opened by a Greek soldier. This was recorded at the start of the recording session, and is a rare example of a sequence recorded out of broadcast order in the studio. The reason for the prerecording is the complexity of the effect involved. Essentially, the shot uses depth as a substitute for height. To give a sense of Troy's impressive walls within the confines of Riverside Studio 1, a forced perspective set was created featuring gates tapering inwards as they rose. This was then set up leaning back at an angle, and shot with a locked-off camera positioned to create a sense of great height. In interview, designer John Wood recalled the actor required to open the gates having to lean at the same angle as the gate set to maintain the illusion[262].

Scene 13 has Odysseus burst into the palace followed by Greek soldiers to confront Priam, Paris and Cassandra. It's a bloodless, smaller-scale version of the palace stormings anticipated in the handwritten breakdown of episode 2 and typed breakdown of episode 3. The opening right side stage directions here are surprisingly technical, suggesting either Tosh, or possibly Leeston-Smith, had a hand in their writing. A filmed model shot of Troy burning is also inserted here.

Scene 14 starts at the bottom of page 22, with Vicki running to the Doctor at the TARDIS followed by Katarina. It's noted there's no page

---

[261] The sequence seems to have been filmed between 27 August and 2 September (Bignell, *Doctor Who on Location*, p16), and I presume the script of 'Horse of Destruction' would have been updated to accommodate Vicki's upcoming departure by then.
[262] Walker, *Talkback: The Sixties*, p98.

23 and stage directions read '**(ONTO PAGE 24)**'. We can safely conclude at this point we are rejoining an earlier iteration of the script. This impression is compounded by a change in the script formatting here. Where previously the Doctor's dialogue has been preceded by '**DOCTOR:**', in this script it's now '**DOCTOR WHO:**', with only one exception between here and the episode's final page. Vicki introduces the Doctor to Katarina, reassures him Steven is safe, and sends Katarina to get him. Entering the TARDIS, Vicki informs the Doctor she has something to tell him. Katarina asks the Doctor if he is 'from the other space', a term we do not seem to have foreshadowed. My suspicion, based on this and the evidence of the changing speech headers, is that we may now be leaving a series of scenes extensively rewritten by Tosh and briefly joining a version of episode 4 that still features Donald Cotton's handling of Katarina. If so, it seems likely Katarina's 'other place' featured in earlier dialogue that's now lost, possibly as part of Vicki attempting to explain her origins[263].

A recording break allows for the introduction of 'Smoke etc.' before scene 15 sees Katarina run through the burning streets to get Steven. She discovers him soon after he's been injured by a Trojan in combat. The sequence would appear to have been carefully contrived to avoid a scene where Steven is forced to kill, even in self-defence. Steven is down and wounded but before his assailant can strike a

---

[263] I base my assumption that Cotton performed a rewrite of this episode on his remark at DWASocial 5, 'I was just told that Vicki was leaving and I must write in someone else.' My presumption much of this work was later overwritten by Tosh draws on the copious typographical evidence I've detailed in this chapter which often helps us differentiate between the authors.

141

death blow he's engaged in combat by a Greek soldier and the pair move off fighting.

Scene 16's script sees Vicki running in tears from the TARDIS, having presumably said her farewells off screen. The Doctor follows, saying 'So young - so very young.' This is not reflected in the soundtrack. Contemporary viewers recall Vicki leaving the TARDIS and hugging it in farewell[264]. It's unclear whether the Doctor emerges on screen.

The scene is clearly very short and is not covered at all in the soundtrack release's narration[265].

Scene 17 has signs of possible revision: 'for long' is rendered as one word; Greeks is spelled with a small 'g' as in the breakdown for scene 10 of this episode. One sentence also sees 'your' used instead of 'you're' and Agamemnon spelled 'Amamemnon'. Dialogue here confirms Cassandra will be given to Agamemnon, as she is in *The Trojan Women* and *The Oresteia*, and sees her predict Odysseus will take 10 years to return from this 10-year war. If we are to trust *The Odyssey*, she's right.

Scene 18, as written, seems to play down the severity of Steven's shoulder injury. Steven is able to speak and the business of him and Katarina reaching the TARDIS is much less involved than onscreen, where Steven is mute and must be busily manoeuvred onto the

---

[264] Robson, 'Eye Witnesses: *The Myth Makers*', p25.
[265] It is possible the brief shot of Vicki leaving the TARDIS preserved by an Australian viewer filming their TV screen comes from here rather than scene 11 of 'Small Prophet, Quick Return' as is often supposed. She appears more subdued than she seems from the soundtrack of that scene and there are no signs of the ropes over the TARDIS that appear in the publicity shots intended to represent it.

couch in the ship. As this is potentially an unaltered Cotton page (the Doctor is still '**DOCTOR WHO:**'), this may reflect Steven's injury not yet being the more serious one requested by Terry Nation, potentially being a wound that brings Vicki to Steven's aid. The single line here in which the Doctor's speech header is '**DOCTOR:**' is the one in which the Doctor rejects Odysseus. 'I've gone far enough with you, my lord Odysseus. Go adventuring without me.' This may be a late insertion to stress the Doctor's disapproval of the Greek hero's amorality.

The next scene, listed as 18A, opens with a telecine sequence representing the plain and the distant ruins of Troy. This is presumably a shot of the model city on location. The scene has also presumably been rewritten to accommodate Vicki remaining with Troilus.

Given the appearance of Aeneas in dialogue and an early story breakdown, I would surmise his arrival was always planned for the end of this scene. I think it likely that Troilus would have originally continued to decry Cressida's perfidy here, until he too planted the seed of a myth, but in the absence of evidence we can only speculate.

The short film extract that covers Aeneas' men approaching on horseback is known to still exist. The clip was taken from *Travellers to Kurdistan*, a 1962 episode of the BBC documentary film series **Adventure** (1961-65) and is either eight seconds (according to the 'Horse of Destruction' PasB record) or six seconds (if we trust the clip duration given in the camera script) in length[266].

The scene's final stage direction states 'THE CAMERA SLOWLY PULLS OUT AS HE TAKES HER HAND, UNTIL THEY ARE TWO SMALL, HOPEFUL FIGURES ON A LARGE OPEN PLAIN', though in the camera directions we seem to remain on a static two-shot.

Scene 19, the episode's final scene, proves an exception to my rough rule of thumb that '**DOCTOR:**' likely suggests a Donald Tosh rewrite and '**DOCTOR WHO:**' probably indicates Cotton's work. Here the Doctor is '**DOCTOR WHO:**' throughout. It's a good reminder we can never have absolutely certainty with this kind of speculation[267].

Steven's injuries appear more severe here, with him now delirious. Katarina refers to the Doctor as a God with a capital 'G', and he denies this with the same capitalisation. Katarina also refers to a scene we've not seen where Vicki has assured her all shall be well. It's unclear if this is a cut sequence or one we simply never got to see, like the first meeting of Troilus and Vicki. Against all odds. William Hartnell's fluff 'I am not a doc... I am not a God,' at the start of his final speech does actually make a sort of sense, as Adrienne Hill seems to end her previously line prematurely calling the Doctor,

---

[266] At the time of writing there is a copy of *Travellers to Kurdistan* on YouTube that has been uploaded by the son of one of its contributors. To my eyes, the most likely sequence to cover six to eight seconds of distant horsemen approaching is the shot 24 minutes and 26 seconds into the upload, though if the clip was indeed just six seconds long, two similar shots that commence 16 minutes 12 seconds into the upload might also serve, if not quite as well. (Stobart, Patrick, 'Adventure On: Travellers to Kurdistan'.)

[267] Unless there really is an earlier version of 'Horse of Destruction' still out there somewhere...

'Doc' rather than 'Doctor' as scripted.

My overall suspicion is that very little of this episode remains Donald Cotton's unaltered work. His lightness of touch is certainly detectable in early sequences, notably those featuring the bickering Trojan royals and Odysseus' observation that the indignity of travelling within the Horse 'takes the fried phoenix', but the episode becomes increasingly tense and urgent as it progresses, I suspect largely through rewrites from Tosh[268].

I hope my attention to some of the typographical quirks that inform that suspicion has not been too wearying.

Brought to Book

We've regularly addressed Cotton's novelisation in passing in the course of our journey through *The Myth Makers* from scene breakdowns to screen, mostly on small points of detail, and I don't intend to rehearse the changes between it and the TV version in any great depth here. The changes can be quickly assessed simply by returning to the book, which rewards multiple readings.

But one thing the book definitely did was encourage an interest in and respect for *The Myth Makers* among **Doctor Who** fans that it had not enjoyed for some years.

There seems to have been a backlash against overtly comic **Doctor Who** in fandom after the more comedic tenure of producer Graham Williams, and, before *The Myth Makers'* narrated audio was released, the opinions of many older fans, who'd seen the serial on

---

[268] A tonal shift highlighted by Jacqueline Rayner and Rob Shearman in 'The Time Team', DWM #292, pp31-32.

transmission and disliked it, held much greater sway[269]. Cotton's novelisation seemed in the mid-1980s to be a bold reinvention and reinvigoration of a serial held to have not quite worked.

But, as we've now seen, access to Cotton's manuscripts proves many of the novel's apparently newly invented and expanded on scenes in fact reflected things he'd planned in the 1960s and not managed to get on screen.

Furthermore, on deeper examination, the riotous, anachronistic voice of Homer that dominates the book turns out to be one Cotton had been successfully deploying long before **Doctor Who** and had been forced to rein in.

Homer's resolute failure to be pinned to one period and his reiteration that he has written a book rather than composed a song or poem (or even a series of scrolls at a push), makes him a modern figure commentating on the action he's involved with. He's a fourth-wall-breaking figure, as much a time traveller as the Doctor, whose playful deconstruction is capped by his assertion that experts claim

---

[269] Trevor Wayne, writing in 1982, for example, bemoaned the 'small, unspectacular sets' and the 'weak and superficial' characterisation. (*An Adventure in Space and Time* #20, p5).

he may not exist[270].

One aspect of Cotton's novelisation that may serve the serial badly, however, is the way in which it deals with Vicki.

Because Homer cannot be present in the TARDIS in early scenes, most of the very little Vicki does in episode 1 is only reported in precis[271]. Similarly, he appears to have no interest in dramatising her departure, with all her actions from episode 4 relayed briefly and without dialogue.

Of course, some of this arises from difficulties working within the strictures of having Homer narrate, but it makes an already hurried and elliptically handled onscreen departure seem even more

---

[270] Cotton, *The Myth Makers*, p107. Cotton may have taken his notion that there was no historical Homer from the school of thought begun in 1664 by François Hédelin, the Abbé d'Aubignac in *Conjectures Académiques* discussed in *Cambridge Ancient History Volume 2*, pp502-03. Hédelin maintained Homer's works were a rough assemblage of material by multiple authors assigned to one name. One rationale for this theory is the lack of surviving ancient references to Homer. Alternatively, Cotton might have been thinking of the theory if a continuum of Homers beginning in the 11th century BCE, and considering *The Iliad* and *Odyssey* to be refined versions of orally transmitted works. This is articulated in JB Bury's *History of Greece for Beginners*, pp36-37, another Cotton research text. Or he may simply have pulled it from the *Encyclopaedia Britannica*, another of his cited sources.
[271] A single dialogue sequence is shoehorned in with the slightly awkward assertion Homer was filled in on it later, and the claim 'You can imagine the conversation...' Cotton, *The Myth Makers*, pp29-31.

147

offhand[272]. In a story that features so few women, it feels a shame to short-change our heroine.

Cherchez La Femme

There is a glaring gap at the heart of *The Myth Makers*, which extends into the novelisation, and its name is Helen. After examining the surviving scene breakdowns, it's pretty clear this is a matter of expediency – the story is already well stuffed with legendary figures to subvert and, as it develops, Helen gets in the way. As the proposed storyline gives way to actual scenes, she somehow disappears from what should be her tale, almost becoming a phantom haunting Troy like the Helen of Euripides.

Her centrality is questioned. She's flighty. She's a pretext for a war motivated by a desire for trade routes. She's booty. Menelaus doesn't seem to want her back. Paris speaks dismissively of running away with her 'as a misunderstanding'. Priam manages to insult both her and Vicki as he compares the two women, talking of it being 'character that counts, not good looks'. She is caricatured in her absence.

And yet Cotton never attempts to debunk Helen's beauty by

---

[272] This may also reflect the apparent reluctance to dramatise Vicki's farewell to the Doctor on screen. It's possible Cotton is more comfortable leaving us to imagine such truly heartfelt moments. Alternatively, if the bulk of episode 4 is not, as I strongly suspect, Cotton's work, he may simply have had less desire to flesh it out in the book. A similarly cursory approach can be detected in much of Cotton's adaptation of Dennis Spooner's *The Romans*. When the dialogue isn't his, he appears far more interested in playing with the eccentric narrative voices that can be.

revealing this too to be a legend grown out of all proportion. That might, after all, seem the most practical response to the challenge of securing an actress to play the most beautiful woman who ever existed, on a BBC teatime budget. The revelation of a plain Helen would almost certainly secure a laugh, but it seems Cotton was more a romantic than a pragmatist or gag-cracker, and knew the power of beauty all too well.

If you expediently never see Helen, she can be whoever you imagine, and, when given the limitless resources of prose, Cotton cast his Helen as the object of every man's desire:

> 'Why, even her hair seemed to change colour while you were actually looking at her: and her figure seemed to flow and mould itself from one sensuous shape to another, like an amoeba looking for a meal! It was quite uncanny. Was she tall or short, plump and voluptuous, or slim and athletic? Impossible to say. All I do know, is that whatever she looked like in fact, the image of what you thought she was would be what you'd been looking for all your life; and what you wanted right now, thank you very much! And furthermore, what you wanted right now, would be what you'd always remember as long as you lived. I've never forgotten her, and I'm going on eighty – but damned if to this day I can tell you why. Just one of those things.'[273]

It seems that for Donald Cotton, the great lover of laughter and ladies, some things were more important than jokes.

---

[273] Cotton, *The Myth Makers*, p84.

A Predictable Ending?

In story terms *The Myth Makers* offers one of the first examples of the Doctor using foreknowledge to actually cause events from the past, by planting the literary notion of the Wooden Horse into the events that inspired it. It's a logical step on from the Doctor accidentally causing the burning of Rome in *The Romans*, that nudges the Doctor into being a (paradoxically) fully active figure in history rather than the observer originally envisaged.

It is also the first of a (surprisingly large) number of **Doctor Who** stories to treat the power of prophecy as real[274]. Cassandra correctly predicts both the arrival of the Trojan Horse and what we know to be the mythological fate of Odysseus. It also seems Katarina's imminent death is preordained (though the scripted moment making this clear is cut before transmission). These prophecies are the first time any form of magic has been seen to work in **Doctor Who**, and no scientific handwave is offered to explain them away. This possibly reflects the production team's desire to prod at the

---

[274] Further stories featuring prophecies that come true include *The Smugglers* (1966), *The Ribos Operation* (1978), *The Fires of Pompeii* (2008), *Planet of the Ood* (2008), *The Stolen Earth* (2008), *Planet of the Dead* (2009), *The Wedding of River Song* (2011) and *Hell Bent* (2015). Latterly these have tended to be dramatically justified by complex temporal science far beyond our human ken. This is not explicitly the case in *The Ribos Operation,* though the production team's early thoughts about segments of the Key to Time influencing their surroundings probably account for the success of that story's seer. *The Myth Makers* and *The Smugglers* offer no such get-out clauses, with the narrative appeal of a prophecy fulfilled trumping any purported rationalism. Myths find a way in the end.

format of the series, and I suspect Brian Hayles' card-reading sequence in *The Smugglers* follows the lead established by the Wiles' team that originally brought him to **Doctor Who**. This does however beg the question of where the idea of the Trojan Horse arose, within the fiction. In later years the Doctor seems not to consider it his own.

Whose Idea Was it?

> Well, it's not my plan exactly, but it has worked before. A fellow called Ulysses pulled it off a little while ago.
>
> (The Doctor, *Underworld* (1978))

One way to resolve this discrepancy might be to imagine the Doctor has forgotten the precise events of *The Myth Makers* by this point. It was a long time ago for viewers, and probably a much longer time for the Doctor. He's certainly managed to forget the name of Odysseus in the interim.

Another way to read the line is to assume the Doctor, having originally learned of the Trojan Horse from legend[275], still attributes the idea to its legendary creator rather than to his own actions which formed the basis of the legend. The idea of the Trojan Horse is essentially acausal, being part of a closed temporal 'bootstrap' loop. It happens only because it happened, so the Doctor can't take any credit.

---

[275] Perhaps from *The Aeneid*, if we want to account for his use of 'Ulysses'.

Who are the Baddies?

One of the **Black Archive** series' regular format features is a short opening section summarising key information about the story under discussion. One of most straightforward fields to fill in is '**Antagonists:**'. However, with the *Myth Makers* there's not one clear set of enemies. The Greeks and Trojans are each other's antagonists and both sides in the fight recruit one of our time travellers in their cause.

The morality of most characters seems somewhat shady and this includes the regular cast. The events that unfold are in large part caused by the arrival of the Doctor. It's his expectations of what the future will hold that come to shape that future and it's his plotting to save the lives of his companions and himself that breaks 10 years of stalemate and leads to the carnage of episode 4. Steven and Vicki both seem to show a relaxed attitude to the annihilation of the Trojans, only seeking to save Troilus from the oncoming disaster, they are, like Odysseus' ultimately self-serving adventurers. I think we could easily argue *The Myth Makers*' chief antagonists are in fact the series regulars, or failing that, fate.

CHAPTER 5: WHAT DID IT LOOK LIKE?

'It looks a little more rough hewn than I expected. Well since it's here we may as well go and take a closer look.'

[Priam, 'Horse of Destruction']

What's Left?

The Myth Makers as broadcast is largely lost. The original videotapes would have been reused or destroyed shortly after broadcast in 1965, and orders were given for the junking of the BBC's film copies in between 1967 and 1969[276]. The bulk of what remains are fan audio recordings of the programme's transmission[277] and copies of its camera scripts. With only a few surviving photographs and no more than a few seconds of moving footage, this makes getting a clear visual sense of *The Myth Makers* a challenge.

Its director, Michael Leeston-Smith, was, by all accounts, something of an eccentric. Donald Tosh calls him 'dotty' while praising his direction[278]. He was a balding man, in his late 40s at the time who, according to *The Myth Makers*' fight arranger Derek Ware, lived

---

[276] The BBC held episode 1, 'Temple of Secrets' on film two years longer than episodes 2 to 4, probably as a result of an oversight rather than it being considered particularly worthy of retention, Pixley, Andrew, 'No Further Interest', *Nothing at the End of the Lane* #2, pp40-41.

[277] We also have 11 very brief 8mm film recordings of the TV screen from an Australian broadcast of *The Myth Makers*. Disappointingly, from a present-day fan perspective, these focus on the regular cast in close up, offering us less evidence than we might have wished for of the show's appearance overall.

[278] Stevens, 'Donald Tosh Interview'.

close to the Frensham Ponds location he selected for the serial and attended rehearsal in jodhpurs, riding boots and a cowboy hat, wielding a riding crop like a 1920s Hollywood director[279]. Perhaps appropriately for this assignment, he was a man with a passion for horses, possibly related to his having served in the Royal Horse Artillery during World War II, and owned a pair of polo ponies, which accounted for the crop, boots and jodhpurs. Peter Purves, who recalls him fondly, remembers him dashing away at the end of rehearsals to play polo in Richmond Park[280], and an area close to Leeston-Smith's polo club conveniently provided the background for location shots of the Trojan Horse model[281]. I strongly suspect it was Leeston-Smith who ensured the stock footage of Aeneas' men on horseback came from a source that avoided the use of identifiable modern European horse tack and saddlery that might have appeared anachronistic.

According to Peter Purves, William Hartnell considered Leeston-Smith a fool[282].

Judging by the camera scripts director Leeston-Smith's production was unusually dynamic and fast-cutting for 1960s **Doctor Who**. Riverside Studios gave him four pedestal cameras, two fitted with

---

[279] '1965', *In Their Own Words, Volume One: 1963-1969*, DWM Special Edition #12, p49; Purves, *Here's One I Wrote Earlier*, p97. Leeston-Smith was born in December 1919. A photograph of him appears on p157 of Brunt, David, *BD to Z Victor 1: The Z Cars Casebook 1962*.
[280] Direct message chat with the author, 20 April 2023.
[281] Bignell, *Doctor Who on Location*, p16. Ham Polo club is in Richmond Park.
[282] Direct message chat with the author, 20 April 2023.

zooms, and a crane mounted Mole camera[283] to play with, and he seems to have fully exploited this. His cameras appear to be extremely mobile with the script, featuring multiple 'developing' shots with shifting compositions. In addition, he switches between camera shots almost twice as often as the directors on surrounding **Doctor Who** productions[284]. It may well be that this ambitious camera work contributed to William Hartnell being struck on the shoulder by a mole camera during the final rehearsal of 'Temple of Secrets'[285]. This fast cutting could be a reaction to a dialogue-heavy script, attempting to add visual interest to what is largely verbal action, but the same aesthetic is reflected in his broadly contemporaneous work on **Z Cars**[286]. The series' adult nature means much of Leeston-Smith's work on **Z Cars** is tough and action-orientated. His episodes include sudden, fast cut sequences of

---

[283] A Mole was a camera mounted on a crane that required three crew members to operate it.

[284] The camera scripts for *The Myth Makers* show 176 camera shots in episode 1, 177 in episode 2, 158 in episode 3 and 93 in episode 4, the latter somewhat short thanks to the inclusion of lengthy film sequences which have no recorded shot changes. This compares to 118, 137, 106 and 89 shots in *Galaxy 4*, 92 in *Mission to the Unknown* and 101, 84, 123 and 128 and 88 for the first five episodes of *The Daleks' Master Plan*.

[285] Pixley, Andrew, 'A Question of Answers'.

[286] Over the course of his involvement with **Z Cars** from 1962 to 1965, Leeston-Smith's shot rate increases, going from around 168 shots over approximately 50 minutes in *Affray* in 1962 to 348 in 1965's *You Got to Have Class*. The intervening episodes feature between 234 and 345 shots. These numbers are rough guides, the shot changes having been counted by hand, and include shots changes in film inserts which aren't recorded in camera scripts.

violence, implied body horror and well-staged and bloody fights arranged by Derek Ware[287].

Complaints at the brutality of scenes in *The Myth Makers* from the BBC's Programme Review Board[288] suggest its fight sequences were also vigorously mounted (though several audience members found some of the fighting 'stiffly' and 'stagily' arranged)[289], and the minor injuries incurred by the actors filming fights on location reinforce this suspicion[290]. One thing that particularly stands out is that Leeston-Smith does not seem to be actively pursuing comic reaction shots in the camera scripts[291]. He notably elects not to favour any of William Hartnell's moments of spluttering surprise and indignation in his first scenes with Achilles, perhaps expecting the comedy to take care of itself while he focused on action, and in a brief interview for *Doctor*

---

[287] Notably in *Affray* and *You Got to Have Class*. There were viewer complaints about the strength of an autopsy scene in *Affray*, although the clicking of a surgical cutting implement offscreen appears to have been the chief cause of distress. *The Z Cars Casebook 1962,* pp156-57.

[288] **The Complete History** #6, p86.

[289] BBC Audience Research report, 8 December 1965, cited in Hearn, Marcus, 'From the Archives', DWM *Doctor Who Chronicles 1965*, p35.

[290] During the filming of location fight scenes, James Lynn (Troilus) was cut on his hand by a sword prop, Cavan Kendall (Achilles) was grazed on the hand by his shield and Alan Haywood (Hector) suffered grazes and blisters on his right hand, elbow and feet (Bignell, *Doctor Who on Location*, p16).

[291] One of the few occasions we do see Leeston-Smith's camera scripts offer a conventional cutaway to a comic reaction occurs in 'Temple of Secrets', when he cuts to a close up of Menelaus spilling his drink as Achilles speaks of meeting Zeus.

Who Magazine, we get a strong sense that he was not entirely sympathetic towards Donald Cotton's sense of humour or hugely enamoured with Hartnell:

> 'I was no fan of William Hartnell and don't even remember him being in my production at all, and if anyone had suggested the alternative story title, "Is There a Doctor in the Horse?", I think I would have vomited on the spot!'[292]

This apparent aversion to comedy also seems to be felt across Leeston-Smith's **Z Cars** work, where moments of potential humour in several episodes feel underexploited[293]. This probably also reflected the tastes of producer John Wiles, who enthusiastically promoted 'virile movement' elsewhere in his work and later articulated a desire to avoid anything 'fey' or overtly 'jokey' in his **Doctor Who**[294]. However, this tougher approach may also contribute to an uncertainty of tone often observed in *The Myth Makers*. Many of the performances are heightened and broadly comic, but appear to take place in a far more brutal world, and the clearly energetic opening fight scene[295] seems to go against the writer's intent that Hector and Achilles combat should be largely verbal and only occasionally punctuated by swordplay.

---

[292] Howett, Dicky, 'Interview with Michael Leeston-Smith', DWM #188, p20.

[293] There are clear comedic elements in the episodes *Remembrance of a Guest, Thursday Afternoon and Happy Go-Lucky* that Leeston-Smith appears to have chosen not to lean into.

[294] *Myth Makers* #79 ; Bentham, 'John Wiles Interview', p9.

[295] The soundtrack features a lot of grunting and clanging under the opening TARDIS scene.

Young fan Mervyn Capel, didn't find the serial comic, stating 'as a comedy it simply wasn't funny [...] I remember sitting cross and resentful as my Greek and Trojan heroes were parodied by middle-aged actors who really didn't seem sure whether they should be playing it straight or for laughs.'[296] It's possible that only having access to the sound of the programme means the comedy of the piece is now more clearly expressed to us than it may have been to viewers at the time, and that the shift of tone in episode 4 was perhaps once less marked. While this is likely down to some of the humour being somewhat rarefied for a child audience[297], this could potentially reflect a mismatch between Leeston-Smith's directing style and some of the serial's broader comedic performances.

A Horse Designed by a Committee

Looking at the serial's designs we find an interesting collision of periods and styles. Most famously, Francis de Wolff's Agamemnon costume reuses the Roman style leather armour he wore in *Carry On Cleo*. Given Wolff's particular physique, this was probably a piece made specifically to fit him, before becoming a stock item available for hire. While hundreds of years out of period, it lacks specific details that stand out as anachronistic and was likely a gift horse that BBC costume designer Daphne Dare found hard to turn down.

The Greek and Trojan warriors all wear short tunics, armour, plumed helmets and leg greaves much as we might imagine, and we see both circular (aspis) shields and lozenge-shaped (thyreos) shields on

---

[296] 'Eye Witnesses: The Myth Makers', p25.
[297] A view articulated by Tom Sloan, BBC Television's Head of Light Entertainment at the BBC's Programme Review Board (TCH volume 6, p86).

images of the set. The Greeks are known to have used both, though the thyreos seem to be a later development. Extrapolating from the location still of Hector and the studio pictures of Steven fighting Paris, we might tentatively suggest the Trojans used the circular shields and the Greeks the lozenge-shaped ones, but Steven and Paris may simply have been given different shaped shields to make differentiating between them easier. Hector and Paris also have higher and notably more extravagant helmet plumes than Steven does as Diomede, perhaps in deference to the Trojans' claimed affinity for horses.

Other costumes have less to distinguish them. Most of the Trojans seem to wear unpatterned robes, coming across as generically ancient or Classical. It seems unlikely Daphne Dare made particular study of HL Lorimer's *Homer and the Monuments* for costume reference here as Donald Cotton recommended, and she would have been unlikely to find much there of use in any case.

John Wood, who recalled researching at the British Museum for his set designs, follows archaeological reconstructions of Mycenaean era sites quite closely for the Trojan square set, attempting to suggest greater scale with a painted backdrop extending the square towards the city walls. The painted buildings here suggest Mycenaean era buildings with sloping walls, angled doorways topped with flat lintels and triangular insets to improve load bearing. This suggests the wall with an arched window used in the Trojan dungeon set may have been an item from stock. Arches don't feature in Greek sites until around the fourth century BCE.

The Trojan palace's portico that stands above the Trojan square contains a set of three dark painted pillars on an elevated rostrum block that appear indebted to Sir Arthur Evans' reconstruction of the Minoan palace at Knossos, and unusually has a visible ceiling, probably to ensure cameras looking up at the set avoided seeing studio lights. This set appears to lead directly into the Trojan palace interior, which features intricate wall patterns painted on a curved backdrop and the staircase already discussed at length. The painted frescos within appear more Classical than archaic in period and in some set photographs we can see complex mosaics have been painted on the studio floor.

There may have been some intent to contrast the opulence of the besieged palace with the more Spartan furnishings of the Greek tents with their rough tables, scattered cushions and triangular stools (one of which is also pictured in the Trojan dungeon set)[298]. It's hard to discern much other detail of note in the surviving photos of the Greek camp beyond the geometric patterns on the drapes representing tent walls and a grand carved chair back presumably intended for Agamemnon.

The use of a painted cyclorama is easily discernible in a surviving set photo of the Trojan square, though it may have been less so when the set was populated with actors and didn't have props leant against the backcloth. Similarly, one photo of Steven and Paris fighting on the plain reveals a clear edge to the photographic backdrop. This might not have been visible on screen, but surviving footage of similar sets in *Galaxy 4* and the billowing backdrops of *The Ark* suggest it would have been.

We can't know how successful the model filming was, though I

---

[298] Walker, *Talkback: The Sixties,* pp97-98.

personally regard Wood's Horse design as a triumph, pleasingly reflecting both archaic art and the Horse's rapid assembly[299].

Wood has also suggested the technique used to depict Trojans moving within the model of Troy on location produced crude results[300]. We can at least presume from the painted backdrop in the Trojan square and Wood's museum research the city model was a fairly plausible period design.

---

[299] Viewers Ian McLachlan and Dene October both recalled the model Horse being impressive ('Eye Witnesses: The Myth Makers', p25).

[300] Wood recalled the shot as having involved a scenic artist painting the city on glass with gaps left so distant extras could be seen moving as though within the city behind it (Walker, *Talkback: The Sixties*, p98). Michael Leeston-Smith recalled a slightly more involved technique deploying the 'Schüfftan' process'; in his recollection, a camera filmed the reflection of a model of Troy in a mirror which had a small section of its silvered backing scraped away to reveal clear glass through which distant extras could be seen. The fact the camera scripts regularly refer to models of Troy suggest Leeston-Smith's memory was more accurate ('Interview – Michael Leeston-Smith', p20).

CHAPTER 6: THE MANY WILES

Given his avowed aversion to the fey and jokey, one might be forgiven for wondering how John Wiles came to approve Donald Cotton's archly performed and gag-filled treatment of the Trojan War for production.

Firstly, we have to remember Wiles' period in charge of **Doctor Who** saw the commissioning of eight Donald Cotton episodes, a return of Peter Butterworth's comic Monk character, and a deliberately comedic Christmas Day episode. This does not feel like a series overseen by a man with no sense of humour.

The truth is, as ever, slightly more complex than the stories we create to make sense of it. Much of Wiles' writing away from **Doctor Who** is earnest and punctuated by brutality, as befits our image of the producer who brought us the two stories that see the Doctor stand by as innocents are slaughtered en masse and the death of two companions[301]. But Wiles does reveal a lightness of touch in several of his novels and the plays he wrote for young people. His comedy, however, majors on character rather than jokes – we are expected to laugh at the recognisable theatrical types in his novel *The Try-Out* (1955), at the profoundly deaf pensioner, old Cassoniers, in *A Short Walk Abroad* (1969), and at the naivety of the narrator of *Killing Casanova* (1993), adrift in a world he does not quite understand. But even these lighter works feature shocking or distressing material, and the admixture of them suggests that if *The Myth Makers* did have its comedy offset by Leeston-Smith's gutsy approach to action, it probably ended up aligning well with Wiles' tastes, even if he

---

[301] Katarina and her replacement Sara.

'would probably have liked to have made it more serious'[302]. Cotton, after all, was recommissioned and we know Wiles wrote to Leeston-Smith expressing the hope that they'd collaborate again[303].

Secondly, Wiles was passionately drawn towards Cotton's subject matter, involving himself with stories relating to antiquity, myth, religion and the nature of heroism throughout his career.

Outsider

Wiles was born Edward John Wiles on 20 September 1925 in Kimberley, a city that grew up around 19th-century diamond mines in the semi-desert Great Karoo, and is the capital of South Africa's Northern Cape[304] – in his own words 'eight thousand miles away in a small town on the outer fringes of the Kalahari Desert'[305].

Throughout his writing Wiles positions himself as an outsider looking

---

[302] Bentham, 'John Wiles Interview', p9.

[303] TCH #6, p83.

[304] Brock, Peter, 'John Wiles Obituary', *The Stage*, 17 June 1999. Brock, the obituary's author, seems to have been a friend of Wiles, thus likely the Patrick Brock mentioned alongside John Wiles in the dedication of Bryan Connon's 1997 book, *Somerset Maugham and the Maugham Dynasty*. A date of 20 September **1924** is given in Locher, Francis, ed, *Contemporary Authors, Vols 9-12*, p960.

[305] Wiles, John, 'From Agincourt to Agamemnon', in Gibson, Rex, ed, *The Education of Feeling*, p39. Wiles is here addressing a UK audience, And there may well be a degree of poetic hyperbole on his part; the Kalahari is some distance to the north of Kimberley. Even so, it is tempting to interpret Donald Cotton's curious digression regarding the Bushmen of the Kalahari in his handwritten draft *The Myth Makers* episode 1 as a passage intended to please his South African producer.

in. In the same piece quoted above, the text of a speech for a 1982 symposium on Theatre in Education, he writes:

> '...because I wasn't born in this country but came to as an alien from a very different background, I have never felt myself to be of this country, in spite of the fact that I have now lived here for 30-odd years. As a writer this has had an enormous effect on me, because unlike many of my peers I have automatically found myself cut off from, or at least less obsessed with the inherently native social and political problems that preoccupy them. This is not to say that I don't sympathise with or admire them for that preoccupation, but it does mean that when I came (come) to look for subjects for my novels, television plays, stage plays or plays for young people, I found (find) myself looking in areas now considered to be unfashionable, even politically unacceptable.'[306]

This sense of being an alien is shared by the protagonists of many of Wiles' novels. Pinto, the Black boy hero of Wiles first novel *The Moon to Play With* (1954) fits in neither the rural South African community in which he was raised nor the city to which he flees. Sebastian, the narrator of *The Try-Out*, is uncomfortable with his family's grand theatrical background, his precise role in the stage company he works for and the provincial environments he inhabits as they tour a play around England. Konstant, the central figure of *Scene of the Meeting* (1956), feels disconnected from the unnamed homeland he fights for due to an education in Paris and home life in England. There are further examples but the most explicit fictional statement of this sense of rootless alienation comes in Wiles' late novel

---

[306] Wiles, 'From Agincourt to Agamemnon', p39.

Homelands (1980).

In *Homelands*, Wiles writes of a South African theatre director, Warren Linden. Linden, like Wiles, settled in England in 1949, and his career takes him to West Germany in circumstances that parallel an incident from Wiles own life. Much of the novel explores Linden's sense of feeling set apart in all the spheres he inhabits, something Linden traces back to an African childhood in which he culturally identified as English despite having no real understanding of the country he felt to be his natural home[307].

Wiles says something similar of himself, when he discusses the culture shock he experience on arriving in Britain in 1949.

> '[...] here was this young foreigner arriving in Britain hoping to make his way in the theatre or perhaps as a writer [...] He knew nothing about the young people of Britain and very little of Britain itself. He had served in the army and considered himself as British as the next man, but of the natives himself he was totally ignorant.'[308]

Linden in *Homelands*, like Wiles, was born in Kimberley, and states his family was of Huguenot extraction. While we have to be extremely cautious about reading too much of Wiles' fiction as autobiographical, this does raise the tantalising prospect of Wiles having shared this Huguenot ancestry, which in turn begs the question of whether the decision to tackle Huguenot oppression in

---

[307] Wiles, John, *Homelands,* pp28-29.
[308] Wiles, 'From Agincourt to Agamemnon', p40. Wiles refers to himself in the third person in much of the text of the presentation, seemingly choosing to stand apart even from himself.

Doctor Who's *The Massacre* (1966) may have had more to with Wiles than has been previously surmised. It's an intriguing possibly, and many Huguenot families did settle in South Africa[309].

It's likely Wiles' attended Kimberley Boys High School[310], before heading to the University of Cape Town in 1941[311]. He then 'cut his education short by volunteering for military service in 1943'[312]. Wiles served as a wireless operator with a tank division, firstly in Egypt and then in Italy, and in his own words combatted battle fatigue with 'drunken leaves in Rome and Venice'[313].

On returning to South Africa after his war service in 1946, Wiles apparently became 'the first professional director and stage manager in South Africa'[314]. Wiles continued to work in theatre 'in rep, stock, and fit-up tours across the country' and in 1949 moved to the UK despite being 'invited to become stage-director' for South Africa's National Theatre[315].

Although he was coy about this at the time, perhaps to protect family who remained in South Africa, Wiles later made clear this relocation

---

[309] It should, however, be noted that Wiles credits Tosh with the idea of *The Massacre* ('The John Wiles Interview Part 2', *TARDIS*, p9).

[310] The school's location, motto and uniform are all given accurately on p35 of *Homelands*.

[311] *Contemporary Authors*, p960.

[312] Gordon, James, ed, 'Author of Promise', *Books and Bookmen*, Volume 1, no 11, p31.

[313] This quotation, along with much of the detail of Wiles early life that follows, also stems from 'Author of Promise'.

[314] According to 'Author of Promise'. On his panel at the DWASocial 5 convention Wiles described himself as an Assistant Stage Manager.

[315] All quotes taken from 'Author of Promise'.

was 'partly motivated by career, but largely in protest against the newly instituted apartheid system.'[316]

A school of thought appears to have developed in **Doctor Who** fan circles in recent years that ascribes racism to Wiles[317], seemingly partly because he was a white South African and partly through a reading of *The Ark* as a parable of Black subjugation and defeated revolution. This, however, ignores a key element of *The Ark*'s plot[318], Wiles' own writing and what feels like an obvious anti-racist message embedded in the Wiles-commissioned serial *The Savages*[319].

Violent Death

It seems military service may have had a considerable impact on Wiles. His later directing style majored on discipline and rigorous physical training, and elements of several of his novels appear to be informed by wartime experiences. A sizeable portion of *Scene of the*

---

[316] Author's biography, *Killing Casanova*. Wiles speaks out against Apartheid South Africa in 'What Makes a City Tick', *Birmingham Sunday Mercury*, 15 March 1959, stating that *The Moon to Play With* was banned there because of its sympathy for the Black population. Linden in *Homelands* shares Wiles' stated motivation for leaving South Africa (pp61-52). Donald Tosh also states that Wiles had 'fled the apartheid regime' in the DVD documentary *The End of the Line*.

[317] Some of the argument's foundations are established in Elizabeth Sandifer's piece 'Ready to Outsit Eternity (*The Ark*)'.

[318] This interpretation ignores the mediating role of the disembodied Refusians, who propose peaceful coexistence to end the cycle of human and Monoid conflict. They offer the synthesis to resolve the plot's thesis and antithesis.

[319] Admittedly, Ian Stuart Black's working title, 'The White Savages', suggests a surprising lack of consideration of the power of colour descriptors on its author's part.

Meeting deals with resistance fighters attempting to prevent the transportation of tanks, *Homelands* features a brutal memory of tank warfare in Italy[320] and the protagonist of Wiles' fourth novel, Steven Chase[321], shares the author's service history in Italy[322]. There's a great deal of killing across Wiles' work, with particularly high body counts occurring in *Scene of the Meeting*, *The March of the Innocents* and *Killing Casanova*, and it's tempting to interpret this as stemming from traumatic war experiences. Sudden brutal deaths, of young people in particular, occur toward the end of many of his books[323].

The bloodthirsty desire to shock apparent in Wiles' work seems to find an obvious parallel during his tenure as producer of **Doctor Who**, as we suddenly discover our young heroes are not immortal, and this appears to have been influenced by more than Wiles attempting to deliver the kind of stories he felt excited children[324].

---

[320] *Scene of the Meeting*, p33.

[321] There are, coincidentally or not, a lot of Stevens and Stephens in Wiles' novels. His final novel *Killing Casanova* also features a prominent Katerina (here spelled with an E).

[322] *The Asphalt Playground*, pp107-08. A secondary character, Cato, the husband of the woman Chase is having an affair with, seems to have inherited elements of Wiles' Egyptian service.

[323] For example, Pinto in *The Moon to Play With*, Gina in *Scene of the Meeting*, Terry in *The Asphalt Playground* and Stephen in *The March of the Innocents*. Other shock deaths of young people occur elsewhere in Wiles' work, but I've chosen to highlight these central figures.

[324] In the DVD documentary 'The End of the Line', Donald Tosh suggests Wiles, through his work with children, had developed a better understanding of child psychology than many of their BBC contemporaries and knew children loved to be frightened.

Reflecting on the depiction of violence during his period on the show, Wiles later claimed he'd wanted to:

'redefine our attitude to death on the screen. I'd always hated our offhand treatment of it when a puff of talcum powder and a rattle on the soundtrack ends a man's life.'[325]

However, he also expressed some reservations over the practical consequences of this approach that he hadn't anticipated as 'a young inexperienced producer':

'I remember saying to my directors and I think too to my story editor "you can't treat death and terror light-heartedly. I mean, if people are going to get shot I think we should make an event of it. It's got to be something fairly gruesome and have an effect on the programme's movement." In fact I soon realised you can't do that on television. It was essentially an entertainment ingredient [...] If you wanted to stop at the mention of a stage death and fall down on your knees and howl and beat your breasts you're going to get nowhere with the programme!'[326]

In contemporary pronouncements, Wiles was perhaps a little disingenuous when discussing the programme's horrific elements:

'"This is something on which we have to keep a sharp eye. What we try to put over is that it is an entertainment which must not be taken too seriously."

---

[325] Goss, James, and Steve Tribe, *The Doctor: His Lives and Times*, p30.
[326] Transcribed from *Myth Makers #79 Bonus Feature*.

'He believes that the alarm which **Dr. Who** may cause among some young viewers is a healthy thing.

'"It is better for them to show it than to bottle it up inside them."

'Many children who watch the programme are deeply concerned about the characters on it. "They always want the good characters to survive. This always happens, and after all, the children are fully conscious of the fact Dr. Who will come out unscathed from the many predicaments in which he finds himself."'[327]

Wiles is quoted here in a piece promoting *The Daleks' Master Plan*. Three weeks after publication, Katarina was dying in deep space.

It's clear Wiles didn't believe children should be protected from difficult material. Writing in 1982 about his work in young people's drama he declares:

'"Sometimes," a [Theatre in Education] person said to me, "there may be doors you shouldn't open." I can't accept that. I can't accept there is anything I must hide from a youngster.'[328]

We might perhaps also see the increase in violence in Wiles' **Doctor Who**, which repeatedly drew censure across his tenure[329], as part of an attempt to appeal to older viewers. Wiles was well aware the

---

[327] Billany, Fred, 'I Drop in on the Wonderland World of the Indestructible Dr. Who', *Ireland's Saturday Night*, 13 November 1965.
[328] 'Wiles, From Agincourt to Agamemnon', pp49-50.
[329] TCH #6, p86, p140, pp142-43, TCH #7, p29.

programme had a considerable adult audience and felt it could be better served:

> '...perhaps I was mad for wanting to change it. But our audience research had shown the Production Office that many adults watched the show, and so I felt we could do better than we were doing. [...] Primarily, we wanted to develop the programme and get it out of the somewhat childish rut it was in. It was the boundaries I think we wanted to extend the most – to push it, if you like, a little bit more towards adult science-fiction; probably less specified that it had been, so we could touch subjects that Verity Lambert and Dennis Spooner hadn't wanted to touch.'[330]

One of those subjects was myth.

Something Greater

> 'We both felt that even if we couldn't change the basic structure we could try to leap further into the imagination. Mysticism attracted us both, satire, deep fantasy.'

> [John Wiles, 1981][331]

Donald Tosh believed Wiles to be an atheist[332] but if so, he appears to have been one of that subset of atheists deeply engaged with religion. Criticism of the Christian church recurs frequently in Wiles' work but seems to focus on either the corruption of church

---

[330] Bentham, 'John Wiles Interview', pp7-8.
[331] McLachlan, Ian K, 'The John Wiles Interview Part 1', *TARDIS*, p22.
[332] Hearn, Marcus, 'Every Child's Favourite Nightmare', DWM #419, p43.

officials[333] or on the church as ineffectual and failing in the face of genuine need[334]. In his book *The March of the Innocents* it's noticeable that he never seeks to cast doubt on the religious vision of the shepherd boy Stephen, which sets the novel's events in motion. Wiles also wrote religious drama for BBC Schools in the 1980s and was happy to appear on a BBC TV religious programme in 1961 discussing the youth work he was engaged with at an institution set up by the National Union of Christian Social Services[335]. This feels far more like the approach of a pragmatic agnostic than an atheist, and it seems Wiles was keen to examine faith through **Doctor Who**.

> 'The other idea that Donald and I had was for a story we were thinking of calling "The Face of God", whereby the TARDIS is stopped in mid-air by this enormous face which claims to be that of God himself. Of course towards the end it would be proven that all was not as it seemed – ironically I think **Star Trek** finally did something very similar, and indeed they did a lot of ideas I would have liked to have seen done on **Doctor Who**, especially those where myth is combined with scientific

---

[333] Prevalent in *The March of the Innocents* and *Killing Casanova*.
[334] An apparently kind-hearted churchman who offers little beyond warm words appears in *The Moon to Play With*, and Wiles' play *Never Had It So Good* has failing churches as one of the targets of its opprobrium (Kynaston, David, *Modernity Britain: A Shake of the Dice, 1959-62*, p41).
[335] **Hearing Voices** (1981), **Meeting Point**, *The Way Back* (1961), Sladen, Christopher, *Oxfordshire Colony: Turners Court Farm School, Wallingford, 1911-1991*, p18. **Meeting Point** was a Sunday evening programme covering a range of religious topics.

achievement.'[336]

This kind of thinking about questionable gods may well have inspired Katarina taking the Doctor to be divine at the end of *The Myth Makers*[337], and perhaps also informed the development of the series' first godlike antagonist, the Celestial Toymaker.

Even when giving a factual presentation, Wiles' language is rich with thoughts of 'prayer' and 'fate'[338] and he seems hungry for the transcendent. His *Lords of Creation* (1987), a play for young people inspired by Balinese legend, opens with a storyteller's assertion:

> 'When it comes right down to it, we are all children of one god or another. Even those who don't believe, make a kind of religion of their disbelief. The name of this deity is unimportant. Call him Akna, Jehova, Mazda, Allah, even the Universal Sub-Conscious... it is all one to me.'[339]

This is a character rather than an author speaking, but Wiles himself clearly feels that belief of some kind is vital to existence, writing in the notes to another play:

> 'I firmly believe that what we all crave (individually and collectively) is identification with something bigger than ourselves, some cause, some theme, some faith that transcends ourselves and gives our lives some meaning. To

---

[336] Bentham, 'John Wiles Interview', p9.

[337] Even though the Doctor is keener to disabuse her of the notion than he is Zeus, this thread ultimately goes nowhere and Katarina labours under her misapprehension till her dying day.

[338] Wiles, 'From Agincourt to Agamemnon', p41.

[339] Wiles, John, *Lords of Creation*, p1.

find no meaning in life is to render life meaningless; I believe the search continues in spite of ourselves.'[340]

Indeed, the utopian aspiration expressed in the final speech of *Lords of Creation* is one of just such a shared higher purpose, as Wiles returns to the image of Spaceship Earth that informed *The Ark* imagining all life on our planet heading out into the universe, united and imbued with some kind of pantheist spirit.

'Proceeding together. The sad, the tawdry and all the splendid things of life. Together. For we are all part of one another, living and dead, young and old, locked in a dream of God who is also inside us and around us. Perhaps in the end the whole of created life will be rescued and have its share in the magnificent freedom which belongs to all His children.'[341]

These aspirations for something beyond are not necessarily spiritual. Another clear strand in Wiles' work is an interest in revolutionary politics. His plays *Act of Madness* (1955) and *A Lesson in Blood and Roses* (1973) both deal with revolutionaries attempting to overthrow the established order, as do the novels *Scene of the Meeting, Homelands, Killing Casanova*. Even *The March of the Innocents*, his book about the Children's Crusade, was interpreted at the time as a defence of contemporary youth protest. The tension between the personal and political is a recurring theme in these

---

[340] Wiles, John, *The Golden Masque of Agamemnon*, p57.
[341] *Lords of Creation*, pp42-43. The phrase 'Spaceship Earth', popularised by economist Barbara Ward, encouraged treating the planet as a shared resource. The central image of *The Ark*, imagining our world inside a giant spaceship, was given to Paul Erickson by Wiles.

works, with Wiles exploring the challenge of serving both one's own desires and a greater cause. Reviewing Wiles' play *A Lesson in Blood and Roses*, writer JW Lambert identifies this as an 'Apollo-Dionysus confrontation'[342], and this tension between personal liberation and political ideals can be seen written large in Wiles' *Killing Casanova*, in which an unworldly French Revolutionary attempts to foment political unrest in Venice but is slowly seduced by the aristocratic society he initially despises.

Stages of Development

On arrival in the UK John Wiles attempted to find work in several fields, working for four years as a furniture porter while writing in the evenings, and apparently writing five novels until a revised version of his first, *The Moon to Play With*, was accepted and published in 1954.

1954 also saw Wiles' first TV work broadcast, **The Dancing Bear**, a six-episode espionage drama for the BBC which Wiles co-wrote with Richard Wade, an actor and writer whose father had been a BBC producer. A further Wade and Wiles collaboration was produced for independent television in 1955, an episode of **The Vise** (1955-57), an anthology drama series made by Danzigers and sold to the respective ABC Televisions of America and the UK.

1955 saw the release of Wiles' second novel, *The Try-Out*, which draws on Wiles' background in stage management. Here a stage manager is thrust unwillingly into a leadership role, becoming, by default, the director, adaptor and ultimately rewriter of a play on

---

[342] Lambert, JW, 'Plays in Performance', *Drama: The Quarterly Theatre Review (Winter 1973)*, p21.

tour. The hero is torn, struggling to serve the original author's intent, please his actors, satisfy audiences and deliver a piece that will be commercially viable, and it's hard not to feel this presages some of Wiles' experiences and lack of ease when producing **Doctor Who**.

What appears to have been Wiles' first play for the UK stage was produced the same year, mounted at the 'Q' Theatre and the Edinburgh Festival[343]. *Act of Madness*, set in a carefully unspecified European capital city, relates events surrounding the assassination of a dictator by a group of students[344]. The play drew positive reviews and was adapted for television in both the UK and Canada in 1956[345].

Wiles third novel *Scene of the Meeting* came in 1956, a story set in a similarly studiously unnamed European country in the hands of a totalitarian regime. Wiles consciously evokes Ernest Hemingway's *A Farewell to Arms* (1929) at its opening, quoting from the John Donne poem that gives Hemingway's book its name on his title page, but this is a slighter tale of personal tensions amongst the resistance.

In 1957 Wiles was invited to join the BBC script unit working as a writer and adaptor, and early work appears to have involved adapting several works by Welsh authors for the screen and an

---

[343] It seems Wiles had previously written a play for the actor Nicholas Amer, though I can find no sign of its production ('His Ambition - to Play Hamlet', *Marylebone Mercury*, 4 February 1955).

[344] The central question of the piece is whether the replacement government born through violent insurrection will be any better than that which it overthrows, a theme returned to in *The Ark*.

[345] The Canadian version on 19 June in the CBC anthology series **Encounter**, the UK version on 7 November presented by Associated-Rediffusion in the **ITV Play of the Week** (1955-74) slot.

episode of the popular light drama **The Grove Family** (1954-57).

A new stage play emerged the same year, staged by a private theatre club to sidestep acquiring a licence for performance from the Lord Chamberlain's Office. *Family on Trial,* an exploration of the aftermath of a schoolboy's suicide, was to be the first of a number of works by Wiles to deal with troubled or disturbed teenage boys[346]. Wiles had been working in youth drama in some capacity since approximately 1954:

> 'Living in the early fifties in Brighton, writing novels and TV plays for a living he agreed to help out at the local boys' club twice a week running their drama group.'[347]

Wiles found himself shocked by the levels of illiteracy he found among the boys, having been raised 'many thousands of miles away in a system that gave ample education if you happened to be white (virtually nothing if you weren't).'[348]

He soon 'discovered he most enjoyed working with those boys who had been in trouble', explaining:

> 'There was something spirited about them. Perhaps it was the rebel in them that attracted the rebel in him. The illiterate,

---

[346] Such works include the novel *The Asphalt Playground*, Wiles' co-authored factual book *The Everlasting Childhood*, the TV play *Nice Break for the Boys* (1963), episodes of various BBC series **This Man Craig** (*Big Fall* (1966)), **Dixon of Dock Green** (*The Run* (1967)), **Paul Temple** (*Long Ride to Red Gap* (1971)) and **Out of the Unknown** (*Taste of Evil* (1971)).
[347] Wiles, 'From Agincourt to Agamemnon', p40. Again Wiles is speaking of himself in the third person.
[348] Wiles, 'From Agincourt to Agamemnon', p41.

the displaced, the unhappy – they soon attracted him in a way no ordinary stable well-adjusted youngster had.'[349]

Through adjudicating drama festivals for the National Association of Boys' Club, Wiles was introduced to the school teacher Alan Garrard in 1955. Garrard was working in dance-drama at a comprehensive school in Loughton, Essex and his methods interested Wiles sufficiently that they co-authored a study of it in the 1957 book *Leap to Life!*. Observing Garrard over a period of months, Wiles became passionate about physical theatre as a tool to help children build confidence and express themselves, and, after observing the boys of Turners Court Farm School at another drama festival, Wiles began to work with the school on a series of large-scale dramas.

Turners Court was a 'colony school' in Oxfordshire that catered to boys the ordinary educational system couldn't accommodate. It had grown out of a philanthropic 19th-century Christian movement which incorporated a certain element of social engineering, aiming to send out boys whose circumstances meant they were likely to end up unemployed or potentially criminal, to labour in Britain's dominions away from Britain. By the 1950s, the school's purpose had shifted. It no longer attempted to prepare boys for emigration and sat somewhere between special education and the approved school system which catered for juvenile offenders[350]. 'Nearly all' the

---

[349] Wiles, 'From Agincourt to Agamemnon', p41.

[350] Turners Court's history is discussed in greater depth in Sladen, *Oxfordshire Colony*, and in Robert Geraint Jones' PhD thesis 'From Farm Training to Therapy: A Case Study in the History of Social Work from a Macro-Micro Social Policy Perspective.'

pupils, Wiles recalled, 'were educationally subnormal'[351].

Wiles' first Turners Court production in 1957 was a one-hour outdoor spectacle combining scenes from Shakespeare's *Henry V* with re-enactions of the Battle of Agincourt, featuring a cast of approximately 120 boys and incorporating the farm school's horses[352].

Wiles appears to have directed with a combination of a firm manner, hope and a football whistle, and to have been rewarded with results, later writing 'Discipline had been totally accepted'[353]. An authoritarian approach to dealing with his casts seems to have become the norm for Wiles thereafter and may not have always served him well[354].

Future big cast shows moved indoors, with subsequent presentations including *King Arthur* in 1960, The *Crusaders* (dealing

---

[351] Wiles, 'From Agincourt to Agamemnon', p42.

[352] Wiles, *The Everlasting Childhood*, pp187-89.

[353] Wiles, 'From Agincourt to Agamemnon', p43.

[354] Discussing his young actors' regime developing his touring production *A Samurai Romeo and Juliet* for the National Association of Boys Club production, Wiles writes:

'Discipline extended to other things apart from punctuality. They were told that if we wanted them to cut their hair for a part, they'd have to do it. If we wanted them to scrub the floor or climb ropes or go for swimming lessons, they'd have to agree. It wasn't that we were a bunch of sadists, but we told them we wanted to ensure that the "thing" was done right. And they agreed. Indeed, the more prohibitive we made it sound, the more enthusiastic they became. (This is not a fantasy).'
(Wiles, 'From Agincourt to Agamemnon', p48.)

with 1212's Children's Crusade) in 1963, *Alexander the Great* (1964) and *Gods of the Sun* (1966), depicting warring Aztec groups. Wiles remembered the cast numbers for these shows were 'never smaller than 80'[355].

The topics selected for the Turners Court spectacles allowed Wiles to indulge a love of mediaeval and ancient history and its heroic leaders. It also gave the boys licence to express themselves physically, often in combat, exhibiting the 'extensive virile movement' Wiles extolls in *The Everlasting Childhood: The Predicament of the Backwards Boy*, a 1959 book co-authored with the warden of Turners Court. The book is a curious read, combining an explanation of the school's organisation, a plea for greater understanding of its boys, a manifesto for the future reorganisation of this field of education and a number of luridly told case histories detailing the boys' troubled backgrounds and behaviour.

Much of Wiles' writing during this time was heavily influenced by his work with Turners Court. His 1964 novel *March of the Innocents* grows out of *The Crusaders* and 1958's *The Asphalt Playground* clearly draws on some of the boys' stories featured in *The Everlasting Childhood*. *Nice Break for the Boys*, a 1963 TV play for Associated-Rediffusion attempted to combine his interests, featuring a huge cast[356] in a story about the education of difficult boys. Set in an Approved School in which trouble breaks out, it was a play Wiles

---

[355] Wiles and a sequence representing a portion of the *King Arthur* show can be seen in a 1960 Pathé News story, 'Boy Chessmen'.
[356] *Variety* reports a cast of 60; 29 of these are schoolboy extras ('From The Production Centres', *Variety*, 20 November 1963).

described as 'a plea for more understanding of delinquency.'[357]

Away from the field of youth drama, Wiles was commissioned to write a new play for Coventry's Belgrade Theatre in 1959, a piece capturing a picture of Coventry that he would research there over the course of two months living in different parts of the city[358]. When it hit the stage in 1960, the play, *Never Had it so Good*, caused a considerable stir, offering a jaundiced view of modern city life. Reviews were mixed, but the play outraged many Coventry residents who felt it was an unfair, outsider's view of their city. The controversy even reached the BBC current affairs series **Panorama** (1953-), with reporter Ludovic Kennedy talking to Wiles and local people about how they saw Coventry and its future.

A contemporary *Daily Mail* review gives a sense of some adverse reactions, describing the play as:

> 'one long litany of protest [...] at false values bred by bursting wage packets, the creed of greed and "I'm all right, Jack", the scramble for bigger TV screens and glossier veneers, trade unions ("they are there to protect the worker from his own inefficiency"), failing churches, Coventry Corporation, and "the technicolour plastic boxes" of contemporary architecture with the emphasis on the "temporary".'[359]

An echo of the play's apparent vitriol may be detected in Wiles' 1982 thoughts about the Britain he discovered on his arrival in 1949:

---

[357] *Daily Herald*, 11 November 1963.
[358] 'John Wiles Wants Drama Designed for Youth', p6, *Birmingham Weekly Post*, 19 February 1960.
[359] Quoted in Kynaston, *Modernity Britain*, p41.

'The war had only been over a few years. Many things were still on ration. Great areas of London and the ports and industrial cities had been laid waste in the bombing and rocket raids. The people were grey and tired and still suspicious of the Welfare State. The fact that you get something for nothing still seemed strange to them. They had won the war by sheer grit. Now they had been promised a lot but because of continuing austerity they were being expected to win the piece the same way.'[360]

Wiles was not a man who seems to have held back with his opinions.

Even one of the play's more positive writeups in The Times felt that it 'presents the sort of criticism that comfortably-situated middle class people like to hear, waxing angry at the soullessness of a working class confronted with new prosperity beyond their wildest dreams'[361]

The play does end up having some tangential influence on **Doctor Who**, being co-directed by Richard Martin, later to be a prominent director of the TV series under Verity Lambert, and provided the series with a new regular. Jackie Lane, later **Doctor Who** companion, Dodo, played the tomboy schoolgirl, Mick Gnobe[362], in a new production of Never Had It So Good for Manchester's Library Theatre

---

[360] Wiles, 'From Agincourt to Agamemnon', p40.
[361] The Times review of 9 March 1960, quoted by Alan Howard, a member of the cast on his personal website.
[362] A role played in the original production by Ann Davies, who Richard Martin later cast as Jenny in The Dalek Invasion of Earth, a role initially conceived as a replacement for Susan

in 1961. It was here Lane first met Wiles, sitting in on rehearsals[363].

Wiles continued to write for the BBC throughout this period, adapting the novel *Pimpernel in Prague* as *On the Edge* in 1960, writing the children's series **Court of Mystery** (1961), drama segments for **Your World** and **Going to Work**, schools programmes exploring young people's problems, and **Walter and Connie** (1963), an **English by Television** educational series for viewers overseas. It's a diverse series of assignments, but as the 1960s progressed Wiles found a definite niche as a story editor of thriller series for BBC2. Wiles was soon keen to move into directing, and pushed for promotion[364]. Instead he found himself given the post of producer on **Doctor Who** (forcing him to stop work on a modern Brian Hayles thriller inspired by the legend of Theseus and the Minotaur).[365]

It was not at all what Wiles had wished for.

An Unhappy Crew

Probably the biggest error Wiles made on **Doctor Who** was the speed with which he tried to stamp the show with his authority and identity. Wiles saw himself as a literary figure worthy of something better[366], and aspired to reinvent the show as something both more

---

[363] Eramo, Steve, 'Cockney Companion', *Starlog* 198, January 1994, p61. Lane and Wiles would have worked together again in 1963 when she played a recurring character in **Compact** while Wiles was its story editor.

[364] Bentham, 'John Wiles Interview', p8.

[365] Walker, *Talkback: The Sixties*, p119.

[366] Bentham, 'John Wiles Interview', p7. At Panopticon VII Wiles compared his high-minded approach as a novelist to fellow panellist Dennis Spooner's as a commercial writer. It's hard to read his

cerebral and visceral than either his bosses or its viewers were ready to embrace. The *Radio Times* preview pressing Tennyson's 'Ulysses' into service to tease *The Myth Makers* with talk of the 'ringing plains of windy Troy' perhaps makes his higher aspirations clear[367].

Wiles was also a man not used to being undermined, whose people skills lacked finesse and as 'at heart, a story man' was perhaps more wedded to serving his writers than taking care of his performers[368]. He enjoyed the freewheeling on-the-fly approach to problem solving of his work on the soap opera **Compact** (1962-65)[369], and Donald Tosh hints at Wiles being a potentially difficult combination of cautious and stubborn:

> '[...] he would listen carefully before coming to a decision, and once the decision was made and agreed upon, he would stand by it and defend it vigorously.'[370]

When Maureen O'Brien criticised her dialogue on the serial *Galaxy 4*, a production largely overseen by Wiles as Verity Lambert stepped down as producer, Wiles chose to side with his writer, William Emms. In 1990, Emms recalled Wiles at the story's readthrough:

---

declared admiration of the latter as entirely sincere (*Myth Makers* #79).

[367] *Radio Times,* 11 September 1965.

[368] Tosh, Donald, 'To stimulate, provoke and entertain', DWM #279, p29. Peter Purves tells a story of Wiles being incandescent with rage at his cast for laughing on the studio floor: 'he couldn't cope with people laughing on the set. He thought it was an insult to him which of course it wasn't' (Marson, 'Interview: Peter Purves', p8).

[369] Bentham, 'John Wiles Interview', p8

[370] Tosh, 'To Stimulate, Provoke and Entertain', p29.

'I had some trouble with the girl playing Vicki. [...] She started saying things like, "But I wouldn't say that," so I said, "I didn't write it for you to say it, I wrote it for the character to say." This started enough trouble, but John was able to pour oil on troubled waters.

'Then Bill Hartnell got stuck in. He wanted to go through the whole script saying, "Ooh," "Hah," and "Hmmm". He was cheating! I said, "How am I supposed to write a story with you saying 'Ooh,' 'Hah,' and 'Hmmm' all the way through?" This became a stand-up shouting match, in which John intervened on my side. John said to Bill, "You do it the way it is or I'll sack you, and if I can't sack you I'll leave." John came to my defence when I needed it most.'[371]

Hartnell was by now struggling with his lines and increasingly keen to distribute tricky material to colleagues and paraphrase in character rather than learn the text. An unsourced recollection of Donald Cotton's in *Doctor Who: The Handbook* finds him:

'sharing a taxi with Hartnell on one occasion and being asked if, instead of writing lines for the Doctor, he could in future simply give an indication of what he wanted the character to say and leave it to the actor to come up with the actual words'[372].

Wiles, understandably, wanted to nip this in the bud. O'Brien's quest

---

[371] Hearn, Marcus, 'Writing **Doctor Who**: William Emms', DWM #156, p13.

[372] Howe, Stammers and Walker, *Doctor Who: The Handbook – The First Doctor*, p51.

for emotional truth and plausible characterisation was acting as an enabler of Hartnell's desire not to avoid learn the words[373]. Wiles had O'Brien written out at the earliest opportunity, but this shot across the bows simply escalated bad feeling. Wiles had failed to communicate his intent to the actors, seriously unsettling the team.

'Poor Maureen was never told she was going. She only found out when she finished reading the scripts that I had sent her, and she was furious. "Why have you written me out?" and I replied, "What do you mean, 'Why have I written you out?' I thought you were going! I was told you were leaving!" And we were at cross purposes for about ten minutes. I'd known Maureen hadn't really been very happy on **Doctor Who** and so I'd thought she'd just decided to leave. Anyway, I then went storming up to the production office, and I said to John, "Look, what the hell's going on? I've just had Maureen O'Brien tearing me to shreds, because nobody's told her..." and he replied, "What do you mean, nobody's told her?" "Well," I said, "didn't you?" And he replied, "Well, of course not. No. That's her agent's job."'[374]

Wiles' decision would have unforeseen script consequences. Katarina, the last-minute replacement for Vicki, held back storytelling and could not be easily removed, and Katarina's mooted long-term replacement, Sara, was played by an actress who didn't want to commit to the series. The next proposed replacement, Anne Chaplet, was, again, a woman from the past, presenting the same

---

[373] 'Veni Vidi Vicki', DWM #366, p17.
[374] Stevens, 'Donald Tosh Interview'.

storytelling challenges as Katarina[375]. Eventually, a slightly awkward means of introducing Dodo, a contemporary companion, was bolted onto a historical adventure[376]. It's a chaotic period of ad hoc rewriting arising from a single precipitate decision.

Beyond that, sacrificing Vicki lost Wiles the team. A large part of O'Brien's job on the series beyond performing in it was to laugh Hartnell out of his frequent bad moods[377], and her badly handled departure made him even more irascible[378], with the situation worsened by O'Brien clearly developing a bond with Max Adrian, the guest star she interacted with chiefly in *The Myth Makers*. Hartnell and Wiles were now enemies. Wiles attempted to replace Hartnell as the series lead, but the actor went over his head to secure a contract extension. In the end, it appears it was management backing Hartnell over him that led to Wiles' resignation[379].

---

[375] Cooray Smith, *The Massacre*, p111 and p115 and TCH #7, p17 and 19.

[376] A stage direction in the camera script for episode 4 of *The Massacre* still refers to Dodo as Anne.

[377] 'Thrills and Rills', DWM #443, p29.

[378] 'Maureen O'Brien in Conversation'.

[379] Wiles claimed Hartnell was the reason he left the programme at DWASocial 5. On page 7 of DWM *Winter Special* 1983 he states 'I'm one of the few producers ever to resign from the BBC, and it was simply because I was heading very rapidly for a nervous breakdown and I decided that if I was going to have a breakdown, it might as well be in something for which I had respect, rather than this programme which, at that stage, I didn't like.' Conversely, Peter Purves believes Wiles resigned 'because he'd got wind of the fact he was going to be sacked' (Adams, Matt, 'Taking the Lead', DWM #483, p9).

After Who

After leaving **Doctor Who**, John Wiles returned to the freelance life, continuing to write scripts for the BBC and Granada, mostly contributions to ongoing series[380], and writing three further novels before his death from cancer on 5 April 1999[381].

Wiles had two more plays staged professionally, *A Lesson in Blood and Roses* and an adaptation of *Emma Bovary*, for Donald Cotton's old stomping ground, the Connaught. The former, part of a season of experimental dramas mounted by the Royal Shakespeare Theatre in a small London venue, drew brutal reviews[382]. Continuing to write and direct for young people, Wiles was involved in a number of plays for the Cockpit Theatre in London, writing four big-cast productions for the theatre between 1976 and 1980. The last of these, *Bush Men*, sees a white South African go to live with a tribe in the Kalahari[383]. Another tells a story of the Trojan War.

Wiles and the Classics

'A number of things changed in 1966. Apart from ending the Turners Court project, Eye also left BBC television where for

---

[380] Interesting curios include **Slim John**, a successor to **Walter and Connie**, using a science fiction thriller as a means to teach English, and a pair of drama documentary scripts for the BBC's **Horizon** team, *The Lysenko Affair* and episode 3 of *Microbes and Men*.

[381] Brock, 'Obituary'.

[382] Trewin, JC 'Blood and Roses', *Birmingham Post*, 8 November 1973; 'In Old Vienna', *The Stage*, 15 November 1973; 'Plays in Performance', *Drama: The Quarterly Theatre Review*, Winter 1973, pp20-21; 'Thick and Clear', *Illustrated London News*, 1 January 1974.

[383] 'Cockpit Youth Theatre: Bushmen', *The Stage*, 9 October 1980.

the past 15 years he had been working as a script editor and- towards the end – as the producer of **Dr. Who**. (It seemed only right that the first adventure he had put the good Doctor into was a visit to the Siege of Troy thus combining elements of the Turners Court. The Trojan Horse with science fiction!)'[384]

As we've seen, Wiles was drawn to both myth and history and he consequently displays a keen interest in the Classics. His contemporary novels are peppered with oddly Classical names like Dido, Hector, Cato and Nestor, and his theatre work explores the Trojan War on three separate occasions.

The first, *The Trojan Horse* (1959), is one of his Turners Court presentations, and little is recorded of it beyond the spectacle of the 12-foot-high Wooden Horse constructed by the boys in the school's workshops. It was not, according to its programme, 'a strictly literal explanation' of the story, being 'a free and creative interpretation of an exciting legend' adding that 'Helen has no part in our story; neither has Cassandra'. The action was mimed to a soundtrack of Sibelius in the school's main hall for an audience of around 400[385].

The second of Wiles' versions of the Trojan War comes in *The Golden*

---

[384] Wiles, 'From Agincourt to Agamemnon', p45. 'Eye' is the name Wiles often gives his past self in this presentation. His stated rationale is that he is seeking to emphasise his role as a witness of past events rather than impose his ego.

[385] All quotes from *Oxfordshire Colony*, pp214-17. In a curious coincidence, 1959's *The Everlasting Child* mentions an earlier Trojan War work having been performed at the school – Drinkwater's *X=0*, the play we encountered previously when discussing Donald Cotton.

Masque of Agamemnon (1977), a reworking of *The Oresteia* produced as a youth project at the Cockpit. The treatment here is brief[386], but reminiscent of *The Myth Makers* in its willingness to find comedy in debunking the heroes. The legendary Odysseus is a half-wit here and Menelaus is almost as clueless as Donald Cotton's version when presented with a model Wooden Horse:

NESTOR

What is it?

MENELAUS

Does it go bang?

ACHILLES

It's a horse.

ODYSSEUS (pleased)

Can I ride it?

ACHILLES

A wooden horse.

MENELAUS

I'm sure it goes bang.

Menelaus even comes close to inventing the Doctor's preferred siege engine:

---

[386] Wiles, John, *The Golden Masque of Agamemnon,* pp17-23. The play principally deals with the sacrifice made by Agamemnon at the beginning of the Trojan War and its terrible aftermath post-war.

MENELAUS

I've had an idea for a secret weapon also. You hang something in the sky —[387]

The third Trojan piece comes in *The Magical Voyage of Ulysses*, Wiles' 1991 version of *The Odyssey* for young performers. The play opens with a depiction of the fall of Troy and its looting by Ulysses' soldiers[388]. The play chiefly deals with Odysseus' journey home but there is a sequence in these early scenes that may be naggingly familiar to fans of *The Myth Makers*:

ULYSSES

[...] Who are you?

ZEUS

Zeus.

ULYSSES

Zeus who?

ZEUS (rather North Country)

Just Zeus, lad. You know, King of the gods, that Zeus.

(Ulysses falls to his knees)

ULYSSES

Great lord! [After a moment] Are you sure?

---

[387] Wiles, *The Golden Masque of Agamemnon*, p21.
[388] Wiles, *The Magical Voyage of Ulysses*, Act I, scene 1, pp1-9.

Sure? Of course I'm sure. You know we gods can take any shape we've a mind to, a swan, a bull, a shower of gold. You shouldn't go by appearances. You know that.[389]

Ulysses himself is presented ambiguously – he is a blasphemer, schemer and trickster, but also 'a general who can't make up his mind'[390], due to thinking deeply and seeing many viewpoints at once. He's also presented as a man capable of change and growth[391], and his Odyssey here represents the process of forging a new sense of identity. It's tempting to see a self-portrait here – an indecisive, overthinking leader embarking on a journey of reinvention and personal growth as he seeks his homeland.

An Area of Concern

Having attempted to redress allegations of racism I feel have been unfairly set at Wiles' door, it would be remiss of me not to point out an aspect of his work I personally find problematic, a strong and recurrent interest in the sexuality of adolescent males and boys.

It could be argued much of this stems from his work engaging with the boys at Turners Court, but Wiles interest in homosocial relationships both between and with boys seems to predate this, appearing alongside several surprisingly matter-of-fact portrayals of bisexual and homosexual attraction in his earliest work. *The Try-Out*

---

[389] Wiles, *The Magical Voyage of Ulysses,* p7.

[390] Wiles, *The Magical Voyage of Ulysses,* p6.

[391] The play shares Ulysses' role between several actors who interact as different aspects of the hero, perhaps partly to avoid burdening one young performer with a huge central role.

features a widowed schoolmaster with a deep, though not apparently sexual, bond with a special pupil, and reveals at the story's end that a sexually predatory young actor and the unhappily married elder statesman of the theatre company both appear to be bisexual and interested in a schoolboy fan of their work[392]. *Scene of the Meeting* depicts a lesbian resistance leader in a relationship with a younger woman who later reveals her bisexuality as she becomes attracted to the novel's protagonist Konstant, while a secondary character, an ex-schoolteacher, is sympathetically portrayed as wracked by a desire he can't act on, for a teenage boy[393]. All these novels precede Wiles' work at Turners Court.

Wiles' later treatment of sexuality is more explicit. *The Asphalt Playground* is set in an inner-city environment where boys sexually experiment during play, men labelled 'steamers' seek out children for sex, and a teacher is revealed to have had a sexual relationship with a pupil, with the challenging suggestion that this may have been a caring act, beneficial to a vulnerable, unhappy boy[394]. In *The March of the Innocents* we find pederastic clergy and intense homosocial and homosexual relationships between children. The participants in the Children's Crusade, mostly boys, pair up, designating themselves as either 'Stags' or 'Does', depending on the roles they perform within their couples. Smaller children considered too young for such

---

[392] *The Try-Out*, p167. It's strongly hinted the lead actor is gay and in a sham marriage but this is never explicitly stated.
[393] *Scene of the Meeting*, p69, p154 and p168. The boy is said to be about 16 (p39) and to have been admired by the teacher since he was about 14 (p152).
[394] *The Asphalt Playground*, pp171-72 and p188.

pairings are classed as 'Fawns'[395].

A Short Walk Abroad sees its 17-year-old protagonist, Tony, both romantically devoted to a girl around his own age and emotionally drawn to Amador, a rough-and-tumble male friend of 15. Tony is later propositioned by an old man who muddles up Tony and Amador and assumes Tony is available for paid sex[396]. Tony subsequently has his virginity taken by an adult woman and is shockingly confronted by a teenage girl trying to sell him her little sister[397].

In *Homelands*, Warren Linden has a sexually awakening at around 12 with two male cousins of a similar age, and later finds himself romantically drawn to both girls and boys[398]. In later life Linden considers himself probably bisexual despite 'leading a purely heterosexual life', having had various sexual encounters with men, and finding 'Boys attracted him occasionally'[399]. Over the course of the novel Linden becomes protective of, and attracted to, a young male prostitute called Tayeb, who appears to be about 16[400]. Linden suspects attempts to discredit him and his work through entrapment are afoot. Despite this he goes on to have sex with Tayeb[401]. *Killing*

---

[395] That these are sexual relationships is very strongly implied. Female 'Does' begin to appear late in the novel despite only male 'Does' having been referred to throughout earlier chapters.

[396] Wiles, *A Short Walk Abroad*, pp196-8.

[397] Wiles, *A Short Walk Abroad*, pp172-74, 135.

[398] Wiles, *Homelands* pp75-76. P122 suggests Linden is about 14 here.

[399] Wiles, *Homelands*, pp98-100.

[400] Wiles, *Homelands*, p97.

[401] Wiles, *Homelands*, pp179-180.

Casanova, Wiles' final novel, depicts a range of sexual behaviour, building towards its central figure being happily seduced by an eager boy named Hansi who physically educates him in homosexual love[402].

There are also strikingly sexual notes in the text of Wiles' young people's drama, *The Golden Masque of Agamemnon,* where stage directions request 'a half-naked boy' who dances 'savagely and obscenely' and an Achilles who should be 'a very sexy young man wearing only a gold jockstrap'[403]. In his accompanying author's note, Wiles is clearly aware there is a line he risks crossing here. Referring to a state of abandon developed in rehearsal through movement exercises, Wiles states that at this point 'The normal reserve of the English young became quite as erotic as I felt we ought to go'[404].

Finally, critical commentary on *A Lesson in Blood and Roses* makes clear the play centres on the seduction of a pair of teenagers with more than one reviewer finding the depicted seduction of a 14-year-old girl and 13-year-old boy (played by the 15-year-old Simon Gipps-Kent) uncomfortable viewing[405].

You may feel I've laboured the point here, perhaps unfairly pulling incidents from their context, but it's the accumulation of depictions of sexualised youth I find particularly telling. This was subject matter Wiles regularly returned to. It is possible this is the area Wiles states

---

[402] Wiles, *Killing Casanova,* p217.
[403] Wiles, *The Golden Masque of Agamemnon,* p p11-12, 19.
[404] Wiles, *The Golden Masque of Agamemnon,* p61.
[405] 'Blood and Roses', *The Birmingham Post,* 8 November 1973; 'Plays in Performance', *Drama: The Quarterly Theatre Review,* Winter 1973, pp20-21.

he was warned against exploring by a Theatre in Education practitioner – the 'doors you shouldn't open'.

It might be reasonably argued there's a cultural hypocrisy at work here. If we're happy to embrace the fictional love of Troilus and Vicki, both stated to be no older than 16 (no matter how implausible that assertion might seem), or take Donald Cotton's Platonic affection towards the teenaged Tamsin Wickling on trust, why should we express concern about fiction exploring same-sex attraction that features individuals of a similar age? However, I personally think it's legitimate to express misgiving when those fictions involve sex between adults and children, even if, as we've seen, such relationships were considered quite ordinary in Classical Greece.

No accusations of impropriety ever appear to have been made against John Wiles, and I make none now. We're in no position to know the truth of, or sit in judgement on, his feelings or actions at this remove, but he clearly wrote enough about sexual activity with, and between, children and adolescents to suggest this was subject matter that occupied his thoughts greatly. If we choose to suppose Wiles' writing might have expressed urges he personally felt, we might also speculate that guarding against this side of his nature might well have contributed to his sense of personal isolation.

THE EPILOGUE

'And what about me? I saw the fall of Troy. World War Five. I was pushing boxes at the Boston Tea Party. Now I'm going to die in a cellar, in Cardiff!'

[The Doctor, *The Unquiet Dead*, 2005]

'Oh, doesn't tempus fugit? Well, I can do no better than to leave you with the famous words from Cleopatra's last speech to Mark Antony, "If you've enjoyed it, please tell your friends." Salute.'

[Lurcio, **Up Pompeii!**]

This has been a longer archaeological dig than I had at first intended. I maintain the best way to arrive at an accurate bigger picture is to start small and work back, but I appreciate this is slow, exacting and sometimes pedantic work. They will never make an Indiana Jones movie about the decipherment of Linear B.

I had initially intended to principally cover the lives and careers of Wiles and Cotton using surviving records at the BBC Written Archive but a period of ill health intervened, making travel challenging and forcing me to rely on reading the authors' own works and accessing local newspaper archives far more than I'd initially anticipated. In this case I feel the road less travelled has borne dividends, forcing me to look beyond the well-trodden data trails and view both men with fresh eyes.

I couldn't have done that without either the excellent research into Cotton of Lucas Testro, or having been suddenly granted the time to read all John Wiles' published works. I'm grateful both for Testro's diligence and generosity and the patience of my editors for this. I think in both cases these have rewarded me with new perspectives on figures I'd previously felt I knew. If time had permitted, I would have loved to explore the work of Donald Tosh, our third great myth maker, in similar depth. Like legend, television is not the work of a single figure, it's the result of an accumulation of voices, sometimes conflicting, coming together to create something greater.

Even unseen, this programme casts its shadow onto modern **Doctor Who**. It balances comedy and drama, the spectacular and the intimate and high intent and low morality in a story designed to speak simultaneously to the child and the adult, that introduces **Doctor Who** to a world of soothsayers and temporal paradoxes it inhabits to this day.

I hope across these pages we've put one or two myths to bed, come to understand a story few of us have seen a little better, and begun to further appreciate the craft and artistry of those who constructed it. The process of exploring the serial has only deepened my love and respect for it, even if it has, perhaps, revealed the heroes behind the programme to be more flawed and human than we had imagined.

There's obviously still more to know about *The Myth Makers*. There are almost certainly variant scripts out there somewhere, and perhaps even more visual material waiting to be uncovered. There's probably evidence yet to come to light that will prove some of my theories here wrong. I do hope so.

Perhaps, one day, even the secret of Cyclops' blind eye will be solved.

Until then, thank you.

APPENDIX: COTTON'S BIBLIOGRAPHY

In correspondence with the **Doctor Who** production team, Donald Cotton lists the works he's referred to in researching the Trojan War.

The titles cited are:

- *Cambridge Ancient History* volumes 2 and 3.

- *Encyclopaedia Britannica*, Volume 22.

- *A History of Greece to 322 BC*, NGL Hammond (1959).

- *The World of Odysseus*, MJ Finley (1956).

- *The Origins of Greek Civilisation*, Chester G Starr (1962).

- *Greek Civilisation*, Andre Bonnard (1957).

- *The Discovery of Man*, Stanley Casson (1939).

- *A History of Greece for Beginners*, JB Berry (1922).

- *A Companion to Greek Studies*, L Whibley (1916).

- *Homer and the Monuments*, HL Lorimer (1950).

I've tried to track down and access a number of these, where possible in the editions Cotton would have used, but now don't personally believe his researches will have extended far beyond taking notes from relevant chapters over a fruitful day at a decent reference library. I probably should have followed his lead.

BIBLIOGRAPHY

Books

Benoît de Sainte-Maure, *The Roman de Troie by Benoît de Sainte-Maure*. Glyn S Burgess and Douglas Kelly, trans, Cambridge, DS Brewer, 2020. ISBN 9781843845430.

Bignell, Richard, *Doctor Who on Location*. London, Reynolds and Hearn, 2001. ISBN 9781903111222.

Boardman, John, Jasper Griffin and Oswyn Murray, eds, *The Oxford History of the Classical World*. Oxford, Oxford University Press, 1986. ISBN 9780192852366.

Brunt, David, *BD to Z Victor 1: The Z Cars Casebook 1962*. Lulu Press, 2014. ISBN 9781326039509.

Bury, JB, SA Cook and FE Adcock, eds, *Cambridge Ancient History Volume 2*. Cambridge, Cambridge University Press, 1924.

Bury, JB, *History of Greece for Beginners*. London, Macmillan, 1903.

Carney, Jessica, *Who's There? The Life and Career of William Hartnell*. London, Virgin, 1996. ISBN 9781781960998.

Casson, Stanley, *The Discovery of Man*. London, Hamish Hamilton, 1940.

Chaucer, Geoffrey, *Troilus and Criseyde*. Stephen A Barley, ed, New York, WW Norton, 2006. ISBN 0393927555.

Cooray Smith, James, *The Massacre*. **The Black Archive** #2. Edinburgh, Obverse Books, 2016. ISBN 9781909031388.

Cotton, Donald, *The Myth Makers*. **The Target Doctor Who Library**

#97. London, Target Books, 1985. ISBN 9780426201700.

Cotton, Donald, *The Gunfighters*. **The Target Doctor Who Library** #101. London, Target Books, 1986. ISBN 9780491037211.

Cotton, Donald, *The Romans*. **The Target Doctor Who Library** #120. London, Target Books, 1987. ISBN 9780426202882.

Cotton, Donald, *The Bodkin Papers*. London, Target Books, 1986. ISBN 9780426202233.

Davies, Russell T, Mark Gatiss, Robert Shearman, Paul Cornell, Steven Moffat, *Doctor Who: The Shooting Scripts*. London, BBC Books, 2005. ISBN 9780563486411.

Gibson, Rex, ed, *The Education of Feeling*. Cambridge, Cambridge Institute of Education, 1983. ISBN 9780856030116.

Wiles, John , 'From Agincourt to Agamemnon'.

Goss, James, and Steve Tribe, *The Doctor: His Lives and Times*. London, BBC Books, 2013. ISBN 9781849906364

Hammond, NGL, *A History of Greece to 322 BC*. Oxford, Oxford University Press, 1959. ISBN 9780198730194.

Heneage, James, *The Shortest History of Greece*. London, Old Street Publishing. 2022. ISBN 9781913083243.

Homer, *The Iliad*. EV Rieu, trans, London, Penguin Classics, 1950. ISBN 9780140440140.

Homer, *The Odyssey*. EV Rieu, trans, London, Penguin Classics, 1946. ISBN 9780140440010.

Howe, David J, Mark Stammers and Stephen James Walker, *The First Doctor*. **Doctor Who: The Handbook**. London, Virgin Publishing,

1994. ISBN 9780426204008.

Locher, Francis, *Contemporary Authors, Vols 9-12*. Gale Research Inc, 1974. ISBN 9780810300026.

Lorimer, HL, *Homer and the Monuments*. London, Macmillan, 1950.

Killen, Mary and Giles Wood, *The Diary of Two Nobodies*. London, Penguin, 2017. ISBN 9780753548189.

Kynaston, David, *Modernity Britain: A Shake of the Dice, 1959-62*. London, Bloomsbury, 2014. ISBN 9781408844397.

Lefèvre, Raoul, *The Recueil of the Histories of Troy by William Caxton & Raoul Lefèvre*. DM Smith, trans, Milton Keynes, Lightning Source, 2021. ISBN 9798475922774.

Menday, RP, and John Wiles, *The Everlasting Childhood*. London, Gollancz, 1959.

Onions, CT, editor, *The Shorter Oxford English Dictionary*. Third edition Oxford, Clarendon Press, 1973. ISBN 0198613008.

Morris, Gabrielle and Jonathan Margolis, *The Book of Luvvies*. London, Chapmans, 1993. ISBN 9781855926554

Purves, Peter, *Here's One I Wrote Earlier...* Swindon, Green Umbrella, 2009. ISBN 9781906635343.

Shakespeare, William *Troilus and Cressida*. **The Arden Shakespeare**. Kenneth Palmer, ed, London, Routledge, 1982. ISBN 9780415027076.

Sladen, Christopher, *Oxfordshire Colony: Turners Court Farm School, Wallingford, 1911-1991*. Bloomington, AuthorHouse, 2011. ISBN 9781452077291.

Starr, Chester G, *The Origins of Greek Civilisation 1100-650 BC*. New York, WW Norton & Company, 1961. ISBN 9780393307795.

Virgil, *The Aeneid*. WF Jackson Knight, trans, London, Penguin Classics. 1956. ISBN 0140440518.

Walker, Stephen James, ed, *Volume One – The Sixties*. **Talkback: The Unofficial and Unauthorised Doctor Who Interview Book**. Tolworth, Telos, 2006. ISBN 9781845830069.

Wiles, John, *The Moon to Play With*. London, Chatto and Windus, 1954.

Wiles, John, *The Try-Out*, London, Chatto and Windus, 1955.

Wiles, John, *Scene of the Meeting*. London, Chatto and Windus, 1956.

Wiles, John, *The Asphalt Playground*. London, Gollancz, 1958.

Wiles, John, *The March of the Innocents*. London, Chatto and Windus, 1964.

Wiles, John, *A Short Walk Abroad*. London, Chatto and Windus, 1969.

Wiles, John, *The Golden Masque of Agamemnon*. London, Heinemann, 1978. ISBN 9780435239350.

Wiles, John, *Homelands*. London, Constable, 1980. ISBN 9780094633100.

Wiles, John, *Lords of Creation: A Play for Young People*. London, Samuel French, 1987. ISBN 9780573050824.

Wiles, John, *The Magical Voyage of Ulysses*. London, Samuel French, 1991. ISBN 9780573050930.

Wiles, John, *Killing Casanova*. Sussex, The Book Guild, 1993. ISBN 9780863328831.

Wiles, John and Alan Garrard, *Leap to Life!*. London, Chatto and Windas, 1957.

Periodicals

Doctor Who Magazine (DWM). Marvel UK, Panini, BBC, 1979-.

'1965'. DWM Special Edition #12: *In Their Own Words*, Volume One: 1963-1969, cover date 12 January 2006.

'The Time Team'. DWM #292, cover date 28 June 2000.

Adams, Matt, 'Taking the Lead'. DWM #483, cover date March 2015.

Ayres, Mark, 'Composers: The 1960s'. DWM Special Edition #41: *The Music of Doctor Who*, cover date 13 August 2015.

Bentham, J Jeremy, 'John Wiles Interview'. *Doctor Who Winter Special* 1983.

Evans, Andrew, 'Script Editing **Who**: Donald Tosh'. DWM #191, cover date 30 September 1992.

Hearn, Marcus, 'Every Child's Favourite Nightmare'. DWM #419, cover date 31 March 2010.

Hearn, Marcus, 'Writing **Doctor Who**: William Emms'. DWM #156, cover date January 1990.

Hearn, Marcus, 'From the Archives'. *Doctor Who Chronicles* 1965, cover date 25 February 2021.

Howett, Dicky, 'Interview with Michael Leeston-Smith'. DWM

#188, cover date 8 July 1992.

Kibble-White, Graham, 'Missing in Action: *The Myth Makers*'. DWM #496, cover date March 2016.

Marson, Richard, 'Interview: Peter Purves'. DWM #121, cover date February 1987.

Robson, Eddie, 'Eye Witnesses: *The Myth Makers*'. DWM #568, cover date October 2021.

Testro, Lucas, 'Man Out of Time'. DWM #581, cover date September 2022.

Testro, Lucas, 'Troy, Troy, Troy Again'. DWM #581, cover date September 2022.

Tosh, Donald, 'To Stimulate, Provoke and Entertain'. DWM #279, cover date 30 June 1999.

'Thrills and Rills', DWM #443, cover date 8 February 2012.

'Veni Vidi Vicki', DWM #366, cover date 1 March 2006.

Doctor Who: An Adventure in Space and Time, CyberMark Services.

The Myth Makers, #20, 1982.

Bentham, Jeremy, 'Katarina'.

Wayne, Trevor, 'Story Review'.

Doctor Who: The Complete History, Hachette, Panini, 2015-19.

Volume 6, Stories 18-21: *Galaxy 4, Mission to the Unknown, The Myth Makers* and *The Daleks' Master Plan*, 2017.

Volume 7, Stories 22-25: *The Massacre, of St Bartholomew's Eve, The Ark, The Celestial Toymaker and The Gunfighters*,

2018.

Drama: The Quarterly Theatre Review. British Theatre Association, 1946-1989.

Lambert, JW, 'Plays in Performance', Winter 1973.

Shorter, Eric, 'Plays in Performance: Regions', Summer 1976.

The Stage, The Stage Media Company Limited, 1881-.

'Guildhall School, On The Level'. 14 December 1950.

'Guildhall School *Pandarus*'. 5 July 1951.

'*Light Fantastic*, Revue at the King's, Hammersmith'. 29 June 1954.

'Witty Irving Review'. 10 March 1955.

'Fortune's Smiles Are Many'. 23 June 1955.

'Two Sweeney Todds: RB Marriott on The Musical'. 17 December 1959.

'Chorus Girls from Convent'. 13 April 1961.

'To Play Euridice'. 19 April 1962.

'Mam'zelle Nitouche'. 13 May 1971.

'On This Week at... Worthing'. 2 May 1974.

'Love Between Friends'. 18 March 1976.

Patrick Brock, 'John Wiles Obituary'. 17 June 1999.

Nothing at the End of the Lane, 1999-

Pixley, Andrew, 'Silent Witnesses'. Issue 1, 1999.

Pixley, Andrew, 'No Further Interest'. Issue 2, 2005.

Nottingham Journal, 1921-953.

'Two Student Plays. Presented at Nottm. University College'. 18 November 1944.

'Marital Comedy – U CDS Present Priestley Play'. 1 March, 1946.

'Playhouse Farewells'. 15 June 1949.

'The Playhouse'. 26 July 1949.

TARDIS, DWAS, 1975-1997, 2003, 2020-.

McLachlan, Ian K, 'The John Wiles Interview Part 1', *TARDIS* volume 5, issue 6, 1980.

McLachlan, Ian K, 'The John Wiles Interview Part 2', *TARDIS* volume 6, issue 1, 1981.

McLachlan, Ian K, 'The John Wiles Interview Part 3', *TARDIS* volume 6, issue 2, 1981.

'Never Had It So Good'. *The Times*, 1 March 1960.

'At the Theatre, "This Word-Play Was Terrific"'. *Kensington Post*, 18 March 1955.

'John Wood Interview'. *The Frame*, No 23 & 24, 1993.

'Look and Listen'. *Uxbridge and West Drayton Advertiser and Gazette*, 30 June 1960.

'Mr Bailey Backs Ten Winners'. *Birmingham Weekly Mercury*, 7 June 1959.

Billany Fred, 'I Drop In On The Wonderland World Of The

Indestructible Dr Who'. *Ireland's Saturday Night*, 13 November 1965.

Eramo, Steve, 'Cockney Companion'. *Starlog* 198, January 1994.

Gordon, James, ed, 'Author of Promise'. *Books and Bookmen*, Hansom Books, Volume 1, No 11, August 1956.

Southwellian, 'Southwell Topics... The New Gilbert & Sullivan?' *Newark Advertiser*, 20 February 1952.

Trewin, JC, 'The Demon Barber at Hammersmith'. *The Birmingham Daily Post*, 12 December 1959.

Trewin, JC, 'The World of the Theatre: A Pair of Villains'. *Illustrated London News,* 26 December 1959.

Television

Adam Adamant Lives! BBC, 1966-1967.

Comedy Playhouse. BBC, 1961-1975.

> *Up Pompeii!* 1969.

Doctor Who. BBC, 1963-

> *Doctor Who: The Collection*, Season 2

>> 'Maureen O'Brien In Conversation'. DVD extra.

>> 'Riverside Story'. DVD extra.

>> 'End of the Line'. DVD extra.

The Serpent Son. BBC, 1979.

> *Agamemnon.*

> *Grave Gifts.*

Furies.

Z Cars. BBC, 1962-1978.

Affray, 1962.

Person Unknown, 1962.

Lucky Accident, 1963.

Hit and Run, 1963.

Remembrance of a Guest, 1963.

Tuesday Afternoon, 1963.

Happy-Go-Lucky, 1964.

You Got to Have Class, 1965.

DVD

Myth Makers, Reeltime Pictures.

Myth Makers #44: Donald Tosh, 1999.

Myth Makers #79: The John Wiles Team, 2005.

Audio

Snell, Tony, *Englishman Abroad (2004)*, reissue of *Medieval and Latter Day Lays* (1973).

Testro, Lucas, *Myth Maker: The Lost Legacy of Donald Cotton.* https://7604971497129.gumroad.com/l/DonaldCotton.

Web

'Business of the House', *Hansard* Volume 217. https://hansard.parliament.uk/Commons/1993-01-

21/debates/a726fc14-73f5-45fe-af3a-7527329eea3c/BusinessOfTheHouse. Accessed June 2023.

'Connaught Show Archive'. https://wtm.uk/visit/wtmstory/connaught-programme-archive/. Accessed April 2023.

'The Cornfield'. Catalogue listing. https://www.worldcat.org/title/1252099270. Accessed April 2023.

'Donald Tosh, Story Editor on **Doctor Who** During the William Hartnell Era: Obituary'. *Daily Telegraph*, 9 January 2020. https://www.telegraph.co.uk/obituaries/2020/01/09/donald-tosh-story-editor-doctor-william-hartnell-era-obituary/. Accessed April 2023.

'Great Britain, Always the Bridesmaid'. *Time*, 23 August 1954. https://content.time.com/time/subscriber/article/0,33009,823487,00.html. Accessed April 2023.

'He Was Joky and Hairy and Bony'. *The Australian Woman's Weekly*, 22 May 1968. https://trove.nla.gov.au/newspaper/article/46075644. Accessed April 2023.

'Hesiod's Works and Days'. https://en.wikisource.org/wiki/Hesiod,_the_Homeric_Hymns_and_Homerica/Works_and_Days. Accessed April 2023.

'Homer And Achilles' Ambush of Troilus: Confronting The Elephant in the Room'. https://www.cambridge.org/core/journals/greece-and-rome/article/abs/homer-and-achilles-ambush-of-troilus-confronting-the-elephant-in-the-room/225D0578715D0F51826D1835855E1036. Accessed April

2023.

'"Horse of Destruction" (*The Myth Makers* Episode 4)'. https://timespacevisualiser.blogspot.com/2017/08/horse-of-destruction-myth-makers.html. Accessed April 2023.

'Mole Cranes'. http://tech-ops.co.uk/next/mole-cranes/. Accessed May 2023.

'Playwright, Actor Had Wide Range of Talents'. *Daily Telegraph*, 28 January 2000. *Doctor Who Cuttings Archive*. https://cuttingsarchive.org/index.php/Donald_Cotton. Accessed April 2023.

'Programme as Broadcast list'. *The Myth Makers*. BBC Online. https://www.bbc.co.uk/doctorwho/classic/episodeguide/pasb/myt hmakers.pdf. Accessed April 2023.

'The Southwellian', 1947-48. http://www.oldsouthwellianarchive.com/resources/Archive-Files/1947-48-Southwellian.pdf. Accessed April 2023.

'The Southwellian', 1950-51. http://www.oldsouthwellianarchive.com/resources/Archive-Files/1950-51-Southwellian.pdf. Accessed April 2023.

Theatricalia.com

> 'Donald Cotton'. https://theatricalia.com/person/10th/donald-cotton. Accessed April 2023.

> 'John Wiles'. https://theatricalia.com/person/44n/john-wiles. Accessed April 2023.

'The Tragedy of Phaethon'. *Radio Times.*

https://genome.ch.bbc.co.uk/fd8b90733b7148c094ff538caf459b67 Accessed April 2023.

Brooke, Michael, 'Shakespeare's Problem Plays'. http://www.screenonline.org.uk/tv/id/1083042/index.html. Accessed April 2023.

Brouwers, Josho, 'Achilles' slaying of Troilus'. https://www.joshobrouwers.com/articles/achilles-slaying-troilus/. Accessed April 2023.

Cistormes, 'A Cautionary Tale'. https://pages.vassar.edu/realarchaeology/2013/09/26/a-cautionary-tale/. Accessed April 2023.

Crewe, ME, 'The Met Office Grows Up: In War and Peace'. https://www.rmets.org/sites/default/files/hist08.pdf. Accessed April 2023.

Evelyn-White, Hugh G, (trans.), *Homerica: The Cypria (fragments)*. https://www.sacred-texts.com/cla/homer/cypria.htm. Accessed April 2023.

Johns, Robert Geraint, 'From Farm Training to Therapy: A Case Study in the History of Social Work from a Macro-Micro Social Policy Perspective'. PhD thesis, 2002, The Open University. http://oro.open.ac.uk/19904/1/pdf86.pdf. Accessed April 2023.

McKay, Angus, 'Angus Mackay Diaries Volume 1 (1940-1952)'. https://angusmackayrip.myfreesites.net/diaries. Accessed April 2023.

Moore, James Ross (2000) 'An Intimate Understanding: The Rise of British Musical Revue 1890-1920'. PhD thesis, University of

Warwick. http://wrap.warwick.ac.uk/4012/ Accessed April 2023.

Parsons, Ian, 'London Revues 1950 – 1954'. https://issuu.com/ianparsons/docs/london_revues_1950-1954. Accessed April 2023.

Pixley, Andrew, 'A Question Of Answers'. https://homepages.bw.edu/~jcurtis/Pixley_2.htm. Accessed April 2023.

Ricks, Steven, *Bonham's Flashback: 7th March 1996 Entertainment sale*. http://www.1stdoctorcostume.com/2017/11/bonhams-1996-7th-march-entertainment.html

Sandifer, Elizabeth, 'Ready to Outsit Eternity (*The Ark*)'. Eruditorum Press. https://www.eruditorumpress.com/blog/ready-to-outsit-eternity-the-ark. Accessed May 2023.

Searle, Humphrey, 'Quadrille with a Raven'. http://www.musicweb-international.com/searle/titlepg.htm. Accessed April 2023.

Solly, Meilan, 'The Many Myths of the Man Who "Discovered" – and Nearly Destroyed – Troy'. *Smithsonian Magazine*, 17 May 2022. https://www.smithsonianmag.com/smart-news/the-many-myths-of-the-man-who-discoveredand-nearly-destroyedtroy-180980102/. Accessed 06 June 2023.

Stevens, Alan, 'Donald Tosh Interview'. *Kaldor City*. http://www.kaldorcity.com/people/dtinterview.html. Accessed April 2023.

Stobart, Patrick, '**Adventure** On: *Travellers to Kurdistan*'. https://www.youtube.com/watch?v=t3f-EBEbFck. Accessed April 2023.

ACKNOWLEDGEMENTS

Ian would like to thank:

Stuart Douglas, Paul Driscoll, Philip Purser-Hallard, Paul Simpson, James Cooray Smith, Ian Greaves, Toby Hadoke, Alistair McGown, Jonathan Morris, James Nye, Andrew Pixley, Peter Purves, Jacqueline Rayner, Michael Seely, Matthew Sweet, and Lucas Testro.

Thanks must also go to several anonymous and exceptionally kind TV researchers, the staff of the BBC Written Archives, the Stocksbridge, Sheffield University and Manchester University libraries, the Classical Studies Department of Dinnington Comprehensive School, the NHS which patched Ian up when this book was first due and to all at Obverse who generously waited until it had. All mistakes are Ian's alone.

BIOGRAPHY

Ian Potter is an occasional sound designer and short story writer who spent 13 years as a television curator at the National Museum of Photography, Film and Television. He's written documentaries, comedy and drama for BBC radio, audio drama for Big Finish Productions and short plays performed at the Crucible Theatre, Sheffield, Contact Theatre, Manchester, West Yorkshire Playhouse, Leeds, and Theatre at the Mill, Bradford.

He's also been paid to talk over old movies by the US company Rifftrax, presented BBC Radio 7's **Comedy Club**, appeared on the Radio 4 arts show **Front Row** and worked as an archive researcher on various BBC TV programmes.

His previous factual writing includes the book *The Rise and Rise of the Independents* (a history of UK television's indie production sector), *The Black Archive #16: Carnival of Monsters* and short pieces on **Doctor Who** for Bloomsbury, Manchester University Press and *Doctor Who Magazine*.

Towards the back end of the 20th Century, he studied Latin and Classics at a South Yorkshire comprehensive, but not very well.